Mick and Nick Nosh started their business collaboration in 1992, becoming renowned for their celebrity parties, after both had enjoyed extensive careers in the media, music and entertainment industries, and apprenticeships in kitchens around the world. Unable to find a restaurant in London to serve them the type of food they wanted to eat, in the surroundings in which they wanted to eat, the food served as they wanted it to be served, they opened their own in London's Fulham Road in 1993. Their reputation for great entertaining and superb, honest 'food with attitude' rapidly grew, and won wide critical acclaim. Following on from their Talk Radio food and drink programme and many other magazine, television and radio appearances, their barbecuing TV series, *Red Hot & Smokin'*, has appeared on the Carlton Food Network, followed by a series on seasonal foods, *Winter Nosh*. Their series *Save Your Bacon* for ITV was followed by a humorous look at the wealth of traditional Spanish food still to be found in Andalucia on the south coast of Spain, *Costa del Nosh*, again for Carlton Food Network. Mick and Nick have just returned from the far north of Scandinavia, capturing the essence of Viking Feasts for CFN's *Nordic Nosh*.

The Nosh Brothers

summer nosh

MACMILLAN

First published 1999 by Macmillan

an imprint of Macmillan Publishers Ltd
25 Eccleston Place, London SW1W 9NF
Basingstoke and Oxford

Associated companies throughout the world

ISBN 0 333 74110 2

1 3 5 7 9 8 6 4 2

A CIP catalogue record for this book is available from
the British Library.

Designed by Macmillan General Books Design Department
Typeset by The Florence Group, Stoodleigh, Devon
Photographic reproduction by Speedsan Ltd, Basildon, Essex
Printed and bound in the UK by Bath Press

Contents

Acknowledgements

We are grateful for assistance and inspiration from the following in preparing *Summer Nosh*:

Kelvin Murray, Tracey and Jo Bennett, Julia Fullerton-Batten, Lucky Smith, Marie Hekimian, Bruce Warwick, Chris Endicott, Michele van Bloepol, Gerry D'Angelo, Bill Knott.

Introduction

Summer Nosh is intended as a trusty companion for the hungry gourmandizer who wants inspiration about the lighter sort of foods we tend to consume in the warmer months. We have included a spread of recipes spanning the food spectrum that forsake the predictable pâtés for the more unusual, such as home-smoked or air-dried meats.

Cast your mind back to previous summers and you may, like us, remember certain brilliant and memorable meals as connected with an event – perhaps an evening classical concert on the grass, a cricket-match tea, or an idyllic spot with the perfect barbecue to match. There should be something for you in this volume that will help you succeed whatever your event, be it a tailgate picnic, a family supper, or a romantic dinner for two.

Summer Nosh provides tips and hints to help you get the best from your kitchen, whatever the occasion, and gives helpful advice for magical results. If you want to compile a menu from our various sections, choose dishes that complement each other – smooth with crunchy, spicy with mild – so there is always a balance, and feel free to take these recipes as a starting point when it comes to inspiration: experiment, adapt and expand to suit your own requirements, and adjust the quantities for the number of your guests. Recipes from each section are illustrated for you to see how we approach the display of each dish – for this is an important part of the appeal, with colours playing as much a part as flavours.

One of the first steps in spontaneous cooking for eating out of doors is a well-stocked larder. Buying some sausages and bread from the super-market is all very well, but stand-bys from your home larder can elevate the humblest snack to gourmet status. Marinades can be helped with flavoured oils (we always keep a ready stock of herb-infused olive oils and chilli sherry and flavoured vinegars as the building blocks of a well-flavoured meal), and pickles and preserved fruits all help to stretch the selection. Another easy step is to keep a fully-loaded liquor cabinet – not just for guzzling, but to assist in the easy application of fluids to turn a dull sauce delightful or a marinade into the delicious (you just try adding Bourbon whiskey to a marinade for chicken breasts for your next barbecue and you'll see what we mean!).

For time-saving ease (who wants to be stuck indoors doing prep when you could be flaked out on a blanket?), get a complement of easy-to-use kitchen implements that will help you speed up preparation. Must-haves in our repertoire are scalloped tongs for stove-top manoeuvring and barbecue grill-top turning, sharp knife blades, and efficient juicers and mixers, but you don't have to go overboard with gadgets – a dough hook for your mixer is a far better investment for pastry making than a new-fangled device that looks good but gets used only a couple of times a year.

Our barbecue section reflects that growing preoccupation with cooking out of doors and gives advice on how to get the best results whether you are marinating, flavouring or actually grilling. Your skills at this, one of Britain's favourite ways of eating, don't have to be professional. A barbie meal can stand on a basis of good, well-prepared salads, cheeses, breads and the like – but you must pay attention to the cooking times and don't try to skimp, and make sure any spicing adds, but doesn't overwhelm. We know some quite adequate cooks who find that the minute they get near a barbecue grill the wheels fall off, and food, especially meats, get presented with a burnt outside and a raw middle – surely the worst thing that can happen at a barbecue event.

Picnics

With Britain's climate, picnics tend to be planned at the last minute, when the weather forecasters say the weekend will be warm and dry. The reality, as we all know, is more likely to be sitting in the comfort of one's car cursing the Met Office or holding a large umbrella over the barbecue with guests looking forlornly through the French windows.

Picnic food is in a class of its own – not simply smaller portions of food that would be better suited to a banquet. Ingredients should be first class, particularly cheeses, eggs, vegetables, meat and fish, and cooking minimal. In this section we give recipes for dishes (such as within The Nosh Platter) that can be made in advance for that last-minute inspired dash to the coast, and we show how to make your own breads – the 'packaging' for ingredients is quick to make and bagels, baguettes, or, as we show here focaccia, are all great for sandwiches.

Use your common sense when packing foodstuffs. Seafoods are particularly volatile and if you are travelling some distance will require freezer-blocks and well-insulated cool boxes for safe transit. When packing your picnic basket, don't be tempted to put your whole dining room cupboard in; plates and serving ware should be kept simple and plain – you don't want to look like a gypsy encampment on disembarking. Be creative with rustic earthenwares and the like, and always remember, white china will never offend the eye with any dish. Enhance but don't overwhelm.

Don't forget the weather is unpredictable and proper attention must be paid to the peripherals: sunshades, insect repellents, and cleanliness for guests if finger foods are being offered. So pack a rug, some simple utensils, and a crate of booze and you're off to your *al fresco* dining experience with minimum effort and maximum style.

Recipes

The Nosh Platter

Electric soup

100ml each of juiced carrot,
celery, mild onion*

1 litre fresh juiced Italian
plum (or vine)
tomatoes

½ tsp fine freshly ground
black pepper

⅔ tsp celery salt

5 shakes Tabasco (or to
taste)

7 shakes Lea and Perrins

2 tbsp mild horseradish
(or 1 tbsp if strong)

juice of ½ a lemon

juice of 1 lime

1 teacup good quality
vodka (e.g. Absolut),
to taste

8 fresh tomatoes peeled,
cored, coarsely chopped
and pulped

4 tbsp chilli sherry

A brainwave of Nick's – he dreamed this up when trying to find ways of getting more booze into food. It really benefits from having a modern electric juicer so that you can get the freshest results from your kitchen. It's a kind of Bloody Mary chilled soup with texture – the texture being provided by fresh finely diced tomato. The classic flavours of celery, tomato with a little heat have been augmented by the addition of a little horseradish for bite and some chilli sherry.

Method

To the carrot, celery, onion and tomato juice add the seasonings, citrus juices and vodka and then stir in the tomato pulp (for texture). Add the chilli sherry gradually, and keep tasting and testing the ferocity of the soup – it should be piquant rather than fiery so don't go overboard on the heat! Serve chilled.

* Using a modern electric juicer the pulp can be easily separated from the essential juices.

Electric soup

Olive focaccia

500g strong white bread
   flour
300ml tepid spring water
1 sachet of easy-blend dried
   yeast
60g olive oil
1 tbsp Maldon sea salt
200g whole black olives
   (pit them yourself) to
   give approx 150g olives

You will need
2 large mixing bowls
   (preferably
   non-metallic)
a 23cm springform tin,
   greased
a pastry brush
a tea towel or clingfilm

Focaccia has yet to catch on as a fashionable item apart from in the trendy sandwich bars of Britain in the way that ciabatta did in the late eighties and early nineties, but in the dominantly Italian-inspired regimes of modern New World cooking it is a mainstay of the club sandwich style of snack meal. We allow you to catch up with current trends at home.

Method

Put half the flour into one bowl with all the water. Cover with the tea towel or clingfilm and leave at room temperature overnight (at least 12 hours).

In another bowl mix the remainder of the flour with the yeast and the rested flour/water mix and stir until well combined. Next, mix in half the olive oil and knead the dough. Add a little more flour or water to adjust the texture of the dough until you have a slack feel: when formed into a ball it should not stay in a ball but rather spread out slightly. Do not add too much flour to make it workable. Mix by hand for about 15 minutes, or 10 minutes in a mixer if you are lazy like us, and add the salt in the last 5 minutes. Round up the ball of dough, place it in a greased plastic bag, blow it up, and twist off the top to seal it (a clingfilmed bowl will do), and let it prove in a warm, not hot, place for 1 hr until it has doubled in size.

Mix together the rest of the oil and the pitted olives. Take the inflated risen dough, punch it down, form it into a ball again, and let it rest for another 15 minutes.

Place the dough on a floured board and make into a disc twice the diameter of the springform tin. Spread half the olive mix in the middle and fold the outside edges of the dough to the centre, slightly overlapping. Now the size should be slightly smaller than the tin size. Place it upside down into the tin and press hard with your fingertips all over the surface to make dimples – you should end up with the filling breaking through in a few places. Now take the rest of the olive mix and spread it on top of the dough. Repeat the prodding routine. Place the tin, covered with clingfilm (or perform the plastic bag routine) in a warm place for about 1 hour to double the size of dough again. Don't knock or bang the tin or surface, as it may deflate the dough and ruin your efforts. Halfway through your waiting time, preheat the oven to 220°C/425°F/gas mark 7.

Place the dough in the oven and reduce the temperature immediately to 180°C/350°F/gas mark 4 for 25–30 minutes. You can cover the top of the bread with tinfoil to prevent any edges burning if required. Let cool for 3 hours before cutting. It seems like a lot of work but we guarantee it will be delicious and worth your while.

Rosemary focaccia

A herby variation of the focaccia theme that is one of those perfect combinations – like cheese 'n' onion, tomato and garlic, and mushrooms with cream. If fresh rosemary is used, rather than dried, you must ensure that there are no woody bits of stem that will render the bread chewy and gritty in texture.

Method
Repeat the method above but omit the olives and replace with 2 tbsp fresh or 1 tbsp dried rosemary.

 **Picnics**

Sage and onion sausage rolls

1 large Spanish onion,
    peeled and finely
    chopped
2 tbsp olive oil
6 tbsp finely chopped fresh
    sage
1.4kg coarse-ground lean
    pork sausage meat
Maldon sea salt and freshly
    ground black pepper
750g fresh flaky pastry,
    thinly rolled
eggwash

To serve
tomato ketchup

The addition of fresh sage transforms this dish from nursery classic to a gourmet picnic treat. They're OK cold, though we prefer them warm with tomato ketchup.

Method

Sauté the onion in the olive oil until light brown. Add the sage and fold into the sausage meat. Season with salt and pepper, then spoon and shape onto the pastry. Damp the edges with eggwash and roll, pressing the edges firmly together to prevent bursting and leaks, and finish the pastry top with eggwash. Cut into small party-sized rolls, salting the top with a little salt, and then cut 2 or 3 slits in the top of each one to help with cooking as the pastry expands. Bake in a hot oven (220°C/425°F/gas mark 7) for 10–15 minutes until golden brown.

Serve warm with tomato ketchup.

Summer club sandwich

1 tsp good-quality olive oil
1 tsp unsalted butter
240g open-cup
    mushrooms, cleaned
    and sliced thinly
1 tsp oregano
1 clove garlic, peeled and
    crushed

1 ripe, firm avocado, stoned
    and peeled
a squeeze of lemon juice

4 pieces of finest bufala
    mozzarella

Maldon sea salt and freshly
    ground white pepper
2 large fully ripe firm
    Italian plum tomatoes,
    skinned
freshly ground black
    pepper
1 slab FOCACCIA (page 16),
    20cm x 20cm
1 tbsp thickly made
    MAYONNAISE (page 21)
4 leaves red oak-leaf lettuce
4 small leaves rocket or
    other exotic leaves

If you're fairly hungry and don't want a typical 'meat-and-two-veg' meal but do want something more than a boring snack, the club sandwich is always a brilliant idea. More often than not, though, there are elements that, improperly done, spoil the gastronomic experience. Like brown bread or bread with hard-to-eat grainy seeds in. Or chewy bacon, or the rind left on so that with one bite you empty the mayonnaise and tomato onto your shirtfront. Maybe the salad is badly drained lollo rosso, tasting like a wet flannel. All the different components of the sandwich leaves a lot of leeway for mistakes.

Here we have used focaccia, which toasts up very well, avocado and bufala mozzarella with a sauté of herby mushrooms to give a strong fleshy texture. The salad should comprise a tasty green element, some mayo and a thin slice of tomato. It goes without saying that you'll need decent salad leaves, and the tomato should be strong-flavoured, without a woody interior and definitely no skin. Otherwise, one chew and we're back to mayonnaise on shirt territory again!

Mushrooms method

Heat the olive oil and butter in a frying pan over a medium-hot flame and cook the mushrooms until the juices run clear, and add the oregano and garlic. When the juices are reduced the mushrooms are cooked, with the buttery coating sticking them together. Allow them to cool slightly and reserve for final assembly of the focaccia.

Avocado method

Coat the avocado halves in lemon juice to prevent them browning, then slice thinly and reserve. Season well before the final assembly.

Mozzarella method

Buffalo cheese is superior to the everyday cow's milk version. It is bought in a bag of saline, and the 'bufala' mozzarella must be

drained. Slice thinly and reserve in the fridge until 5 minutes before the assembly.

Salad method

Using fresh ingredients ensures a good result. Red oak-leaf lettuce or batavia is decent although you can get new exotic salad leaves like shungiko (a dwarf chrysanthemum) and mizuna, or the very esoteric types like texel, tatsai, gold orach, serrated santo, celtuce and jaba. A little rocket is fine but don't use too much or the taste will dominate the dish. Green salad should be picked clean, washed and drained. It is vital that it is dry and that the tomatoes are skinned and sliced thinly.

- One of our favourite tastes is young pea shoots – pea seeds, sprouted and grown to a height of about 3–4 inches and then cropped. They have all the juicy sweetness of the pea flavour with crunchy, juicy leaves.
- Always try to use young leaves, older ones have a coarseness you don't want.
- When washing leaves, replenish the water several times: it only takes one piece of grit to spoil the whole dish. And remember to drain and dry them thoroughly – a toss in a dry tea towel is quite effective if you're in a hurry.
- Cut the leaves, don't tear them: tearing causes the edges of the leaves to oxidize and go brown. Remember not to toss in the dressing until you need to serve – otherwise it will wilt the leaves.

Don't use lollo rosso. It is a limp-wristed tasteless lettuce that will not enhance any salad (although lollo biancho, the plain 'green' version, is not too bad).

If you're using purslane, radicchio, claytonia, or frisée (curly endive) be very sparing, as these leaves have a bitter or sour taste and will dominate the sandwich flavours.

Assembly

Toast the focaccia lightly on both sides and cut it horizontally into three equal slices. Spread a thin layer of mayo on the cut edges of the top and bottom slices and both sides of the middle slice. (This is the glue that holds it all together.) Try building up from the bottom up with layers thus (but don't be afraid to vary the combinations as you wish):

focaccia, mayo, oak-leaf lettuce, tomato, seasoning, mozzarella, rocket, avocado slices, seasoning, mayo, focaccia, mayo, oak-leaf lettuce, tomato, seasoning, oregano mushrooms, rocket, mayo, focaccia.

Mayonnaise

Makes about 600ml

3 small egg yolks*
1 tbsp white wine vinegar
300ml best-quality olive oil
300ml good-quality salad
    oil (sunflower, etc., but
    not soya)
Maldon sea salt
1 tsp good-quality Dijon
    mustard
1 tsp lemon juice
freshly ground black
    pepper
a pinch of caster sugar

Mayo was invented by the Duc de Richelieu's chef in 1756 in Port Mahon, Minorca (we take our hats off to him), and on any modern Spanish street they still have some of the greatest stuff in the restaurants and tapas bars. (Even the plastic containers with the industrially-made versions are pretty good and put most English-produced offerings to shame.) It's not surprising, really, as the Spanish mainly export their second-grade olive oils to Britain, leaving the prime-quality ones (below 1 per cent acidity) for the home market. For best home-made results, always use the best and freshest ingredients you can get your hands on.

Method

Mix the oils. Whisk the egg yolks with some salt and the mustard, then drizzle in half the mixed oils, incorporating them thoroughly and beating all the time. Then add the lemon juice and continue to pour and whisk oil in. Finally adjust the seasoning, adding salt, pepper and sugar if necessary. If the mayonnaise looks too thin or has split and curdled, it is possible to rescue it by beating another yolk in a separate bowl and pouring the original mixture in gradually, beating well as before, but really taking plenty of time to whisk well together.

* To remove the worries and fears about any lurking salmonella in raw egg, simply mix the yolks with the vinegar at the start and leave for 5–10 minutes, stirring once or twice. Salmonella hate vinegar and it will reduce the risk of any contamination.

 **Picnics**

The Nosh Platter

'The Nosh Platter' has a history that stretches back to the balmy days of our restaurant in the Fulham Road during the early and mid-nineties. We would offer the platter on the starter section of our daily menu that would, in effect, be a smorgasbord of savoury items that offered a seasonal taste of our Nosh style of cuisine. It would have contained smoked fish or meats, grilled vegetables, home-made breads, dips or any gourmet titbits that we deemed fitting for the spread. It was, in essence, a kind of Nosh version of the Mediterranean antipasto and we became rightly famed for a generous offering that would not have looked out of place on a Sicilian Don's family picnic. The Nosh Platter was always sold as 'for two people' to share (although tough eaters devoured it with ease) and soon became very popular. The benefits for us, as restaurateurs, was that as we operated as a small brasserie, the menu largely changed every day – just as in an Italian trattoria – and small items left from the previous lunchtime, perhaps a few slices of fresh-grilled tuna or some bresaola, too few to be included as a separate item on the main menu, would be presented in this fashion and economically consumed the same day.

Here we have specified some famous Platter items that were always popular, particularly the smoked meats – duck breast in this case, bresaola and a new addition reaped from our travels to Spain, *confitat* of pork (a Spanish version of *confit* using pork fillet and lard as a cooking and preserving medium).

It should be noted, however, that you do not have to organize a picnic to enjoy the tastes we have listed here. Smoking, drying and preserving meats simply ensures that you do not suffer the panic of 'what do I make. . . ?' if guests call unexpectedly – with tasty marinated and smoked and dried items with a long shelf-life you always have a tasty repertoire to offer them without having to start rolling your sleeves up – especially when, like us, you'd rather be sipping a gin and tonic with friends.

Sardine crostinis with tapenade

Serves 1

2 slices thick-cut CIABATTA
    (page 65)
1 clove garlic, crushed
virgin olive oil
TAPENADE
2 fresh sardines
1 tsp olive oil
Maldon sea salt and freshly
    ground black pepper

To serve
wedges of lemon

Sardines of the tinned kind are as English as roast beef and the White Cliffs of Dover. They have a sort of Spartan feel to them and are often relegated to the back shelf of the kitchen cupboard as 'emergency' food. On the other hand, as anyone who has had a Mediterranean holiday knows, freshly grilled they can be a gourmet delight.

Fresh sardines are a naturally oily fish and lend themselves easily to the grill or barbecue. Choosing largish ones will make the exercise of taking them off the bone easy. Here, we have modernized the traditional 'whales on toast' by presenting them on ciabatta with a tapenade to give a piquant edge.

Method
Brush the ciabatta with the garlic and olive oil, toast it lightly, and then smear with a dab of tapenade.

Wash the sardines free of any stray scales or gunk and drain dry on kitchen paper. Paint them with olive oil, season and grill for 3–5 minutes turning them once until the flesh is cooked, then, using a very sharp knife, cut down the spine of each sardine, free the fillet from the backbone, and place on the ciabatta. A quick squeeze of lemon will complete this simple but majestic-tasting dish.

1 small tin drained
    anchovies
3 cloves peeled, chopped
    garlic
1 small jar pitted black
    olives (Greek Kalamatas
    are good)
2 tbsp drained pickled
    caper berries
2 tbsp good virgin olive oil

Tapenade

Method
Place the ingredients in a food processor and blitz on pulse for a few short bursts. You should not purée them but end up with a coarse, oily pâté-like mix.

Fillet of beef bresaola

Makes enough for 16

½ bottle red wine
½ bottle white wine
600g salt
4 cloves garlic, peeled and
    crushed
1 stick cinnamon
6 whole cloves
16 black peppercorns
6 bay leaves
2 large sprigs rosemary
2 large sprigs thyme
4 dried chillies
zest of 1 orange
1.2kg best Scotch fillet,
    trimmed of all fat and
    sinews

To serve
Parmesan cheese
or
INFUSED LEMON OIL

Bresaola is essentially raw fillet of beef that has been cured in brine then air-dried, ready to be eaten within a couple of months. In principle, it is similar to Parma ham, a dried fully-flavoured cured meat with a dryish texture, but the taste is more delicate and the texture a little more robust than any prosciutto. Traditionally from the valleys of Lombardy, it is served at serious dinners as an 'antipasto' starter, usually with some form of lemon-infused olive oil or shaved Parmesan and black pepper.

Curing the beef is a combination of 'corning' it (that is, salting it in brine) and marinating it in wine as you would for a pot-roast.

Method

Pour the wine into a large basin and stir in the salt until all the salt is dissolved. Then add the garlic, spices, herbs, chillies, and orange zest and place the fillet in the liquid so that the surface is well covered by the liquid. Cover the bowl with clingfilm and place it in the fridge for a week. The brine mixture will take out most of the meat's excess moisture; it can then be discarded. Take out the beef and drain it, pat it dry with a sterile kitchen cloth or tea towel, wrap it in a clean muslin cloth and hang it in a cool well-ventilated place like a cold larder for another week. This will dry out the outside of the joint and render the overall texture more dense and not unlike Parma ham. Finally, rub the outside of the joint with some olive oil, which will prevent the outer skin hardening off further. The beef can then be sliced wafer-thin until a couple of centimetres or so of 'end' has been removed, revealing the more moist inner core of meat. The slices must be kept thin as the meat is still quite chewy. Dress the slices with shavings of Reggiano Parmesan cheese or infused lemon oil.

Infused lemon oil

You can buy ready-made lemon-infused olive oil ready for pouring, but it's easily made at home.

Simply blanch whole fresh lemons in boiling water for a few minutes (this enables any residual waxy coating to be cleaned off with a dry cloth and ensures a sterile outer skin) then cut into wedges and push them into a sterile clear glass bottle (an old empty olive oil bottle is fine). The best oil to use is a medium-weight olive oil that has a smooth, even light, not peppery, flavour. (Some of the greeny virgin first pressings are too strong in flavour and will mask the delicacy of your dish.) Cap the bottle with a stainless steel and cork drinks pourer and you will have a lemon oil for dressing fish or other foods within a week. So long as you can keep the lemon slices immersed in the oil, they will not get furry with mildew. The flavour can be further accentuated by steeping peeled inner stems of lemon grass in the oil, which gives an oriental taste.

For 12 portions

6 large 'free-range'* pork
    fillets, larder trimmed
4 tbsp olive oil
6 dried Espelette pimientos
1 litre melted lard

Confitat of pork fillet with Espelette pimientos

Confitat is the Spanish version of *confit*, and it is prevalent in the Catalan and Basque regions. Just on the other side of the border, in France, there is a town called Espelette, famous for its medium-hot red pimientos. They use them in almost all their cooking including the flavouring of their Bayonne hams, which are sadly, inferior to the Spanish *jamons Serranos*. In Espelette they have a speciality, adapting the Spanish taste for fillet of pork *confitat* in pork fat or lard, by combining both of the two ingredients – the fantastic Espelette peppers with the great *lomo* or pork meat of Spain. Whereas France favours goose fat for its confits, Spain uses lard, which it has in plentiful supply. Don't be put off by the degree of fat used here – remember, it is used for *preserving* the lean meat, and once grilled the dish will not appear unduly rich.

Method

Ensure each pork fillet is free of all fat, connective tissue and sinew. (If the butcher hasn't done it, you will need to remove the pencil-thick chain, the connective strip of flesh that runs along the side of the fillet.) Then brush and rub olive oil into each one.

Crush the dried peppers (these give a medium warm 'heat' to a dish, halfway between chillies and sweet bell peppers) and blitz them in a blender to give a coarse powder. Rub the fillets evenly, cover them with clingfilm, and chill for 24 hours to let the flavours of the pimientos seep into the pork.

Next day, heat the lard to about 140°C/275°F in a deep-frying saucepan or electric fryer and when it starts to bubble and crackle

In Spain, the exquisite flavour of the pork is provided by a free-ranging diet, which traditionally contained acorns. It may be difficult to source a similar type but try to get the best. (The more varied the animal's diet, the more varied the flavour.)

simmer the pork for 30 minutes at just under a slow bubble, then remove with tongs. Place it in a sterile plastic container and cover with the molten pork fat, ensuring that all the meat is submerged under the surface, and leave in a cool place to solidify. The fat will congeal when cool and seal the meats and preserve them.

Any meat juices that escape from the fillets during the *confitat* process will accumulate at the bottom of the fatty layer, resembling a meaty jelly. It can be removed with a spoon – it will be very useful and tasty for adding to your gravies or stocks. The fillets can be safely kept for a couple of months, if sealed by fat and refrigerated. The fat can be used again up to four times, gaining flavour and improving the final result.

When you want to cook a fillet, wipe it clean of fat and grill it over a very high flame for 5 minutes – barbecuing is very effective.

Smoked breast of duck, with ginger

Makes 12 portions

4 magret breasts of duck
3 tsp dried ground ginger
small pinch Maldon sea salt
2 tbsp stem ginger syrup
1 tbsp olive oil
½ tsp ground anise

You will need
for smoking
a small metal sieve
a foil tray of the same size
a large metal tray with high
   sides
charcoal/wood chips

Hot-smoking the duck can be easily done at home in the oven – you don't need special equipment. (Ensure that the kitchen is well ventilated, as charcoal issues carbon monoxide fumes that should not be inhaled.)

Method
Trim the duck breasts of all surplus fat and skin, leaving a smallish inner covering of skin (prick the skin with a skewer and criss-cross the surface with a sharp knife to allow any excess fats to roast off during hot-smoking). Then in a wide shallow bowl mix the ginger, salt, ginger syrup, olive oil and anise into a thick syrup and smear over all the surfaces of the meat. Rest in the marinade for 4 hours then seasoned if desired. Oiling lightly with seasonings and spices gives a piquant flavour to the meat – but don't overdo it. The spice should not mask the smoky element.

Smoke in the oven according to the following method.

Smoking method
The idea here is to simply heat some charcoal, placing it in a large-mesh metal sieve over a hot flame until combusting and then sprinkle over some woodchips (previously soaked overnight in water) to create the smoke. Place it in the bottom of a preheated oven (180°C/350°F/gas mark 4) in a foil tray, and arrange it below a wire tray of duck breasts, covered with a foil lid (to hold the smoke in) punched with a couple of slits for venting. Ensure that the small charcoal dish is to one side of the large tray, otherwise the duck juices will drip onto the hot coals as they cook, and extinguish them. The breasts can then be hot-smoked for about 20–25 minutes depending on size. When cooked the interior should look moist when sliced through, but not actually bloody, although a slight hint of pink is OK.

When the breasts have cooled down, they can be very thinly sliced and arranged as part of The Nosh Platter or a starter plate of charcuterie for that impromptu late supper or lunch when guests call unexpectedly. (See also the recipes for Fillet of beef bresaola, page 24, and *Confitat* of pork fillet, page 26.)

Marinated olives

Serves 6–8

230g green or black olives*
½ tsp ground cumin
½ tsp oregano (or 1 tbsp chopped marjoram if you can get it)
½ tsp chopped rosemary
½ tsp chopped thyme
½ tsp fennel seeds
4 bay leaves
6 cloves garlic, peeled
1 tbsp sherry vinegar
1 tbsp lemon juice

Olives are naturally a bitter fruit. That's why they need to be marinated in brine and refreshed in many changes of water to arrive at a palatable product. They tend to be a love it or hate it kind of thing (we love it) that benefits from extra infusions of flavour to make great aperitif nibbles with a full-on impact on the taste buds. Here we use garlic, herbs and spices to transform them.

Method
Place all the ingredients mixed together in a large Kilner-type preserving jar and screw or clip the lid down firmly. Top up with a few tablespoonsful of olive oil if needed and rotate the jar every few days, agitating the contents to spread the flavours throughout. Kept at room temperature, the olives will reach decent levels of flavour after 3–4 days.

* Ensure that if black, they are not pitted. True black olives are well-ripened ones that are too soft in texture to allow easy pitting. The supermarket pitted black olives are frauds. They are green pitted olives that have had a makeover with food colourings to masquerade as black. Avoid them at all costs.

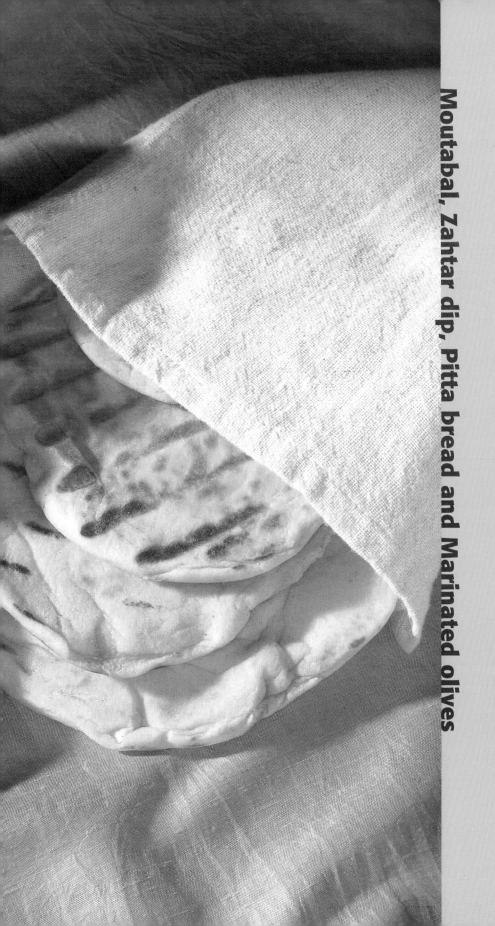

Moutabal, Zahtar dip, Pitta bread and Marinated olives

Pitta bread

450g strong white bread
  flour
1 level tsp Maldon sea salt
1 sachet easy-blend dried
  yeast
300ml lukewarm water
3 tbsp olive oil

Everyone knows the distinctive flat oval of pitta bread that accompanies most Middle Eastern starters. This flat disc with all the appeal of a savoury beermat bears no relation to the aromatic pockets of pittas baked on a metal dome over an open charcoal fire. Realistically, we cannot reproduce this at home so we'll have to make do with a domestic oven. The effort is well worth it and has more importance in the process of self-indulgence than merely 'filling the gap'.

Pieces of bread can be broken off and used to envelop a tasty morsel of meat or scoop up some pâté, such as hummus, moutabal or zahtar; if you're in a hurry it can be split in two and stuffed to make a takeaway for a handy snack. Finally, it's without question the best way of mopping up the juices left on the plate at the end of a meal. Dispense with niceties, and dip yer bread in!

Method

Sift the flour, salt and yeast into a bowl and make a well in the centre. Add the water and oil to make a dough, and work it well on a floured board until it is smooth, shiny and elastic. 10–15 minutes should give a good result, but if you are lucky enough to have an electric mixer with bread-dough hook, 5 minutes will be enough. Smear the dough with a little extra oil and let it rest in the bowl, in a warm place, covered with clingfilm, for 1–2 hours or until it has doubled in size.

Next, take a piece of risen dough the size of your fist and flatten it on a lightly floured surface first with your hand and then with a floured rolling pin until it is about 5mm thick. Dust with extra flour and lay on a floured tray in a warm place to rise again (to prove) for 30 minutes, and preheat your oven to maximum (at least 230°C/450°F/gas mark 8).

Place lightly oiled heavy-based baking trays in the oven for 5 minutes so the metal is very hot. Slip the flat rounds of dough onto them, and bake for about 10 minutes (without opening the oven door): as they bake the breads should puff up so that a natural pouch forms inside. Cool them on a wire rack.

They are best eaten fresh from the hot oven, but to reheat them simply toast in an electric toaster or wrap them in foil and put them in a warm oven for a few minutes.

Moutabal

Serves 6

3 large aubergines
3 cloves garlic
Maldon sea salt
150ml tahina paste
juice of 3 lemons
4 tbsp virgin olive oil
½ tsp ground cumin
2 tbsp finely chopped flat-
 leaf parsley

To serve
PITTA BREAD
virgin olive oil
chopped olives
toasted whole cumin seeds

This is a dip with aubergine, sharpened by the addition of lemon and garlic and the strong taste of tahina. Don't worry if you burn the aubergines slightly, the tiny specks of any blistered skin that remains will add a smoky taste to the paste that enhances the flavour.

Method
Roast the aubergines in a preheated oven (220°C/425°F/gas mark 7) until the skin blisters and shrivels and the centre of the aubergine is cooked through (about 40 minutes). Peel the skin off and reserve the pulped flesh.

Crush the garlic with salt and add to the aubergine pulp. Add the tahina, lemon juice, and olive oil and and whip up into a smooth purée. Add the cumin and parsley and adjust the seasoning.

Serve in flat dishes with toasted flat bread (Lebanese or pitta), garnished with olive oil, olives and a sprinkle of toasted cumin seeds.

Zahtar dip for breads

30g toasted sesame seeds

30g pulverized sesame seeds

1 tsp pulverized Maldon sea salt

1 tsp dried thyme

½ tsp freshly ground black pepper

½ tsp cumin seeds

1 tsp sumac (or *summak*), powdered*

2 tbsp virgin olive oil

A traditional Middle Eastern seasoning for breads is called zahtar (pronounced 'sach-turr'), toasted sesame seeds, crushed with salt and a little dried thyme, and spices. This can be sprinkled over the breads as they come out of the oven, or it can be dipped into as a condiment with the addition of a little virgin olive oil to mix it into a paste.

Method

Mix all the dry ingredients together and add the oil to make a paste. Dipping the hot bread in makes it perfect for a Middle Eastern style relish.

* Sumac is a sourish, dark brown/red seed which can be easily obtained from Iranian and Egyptian/Lebanese delis. Iraqis use it frequently and the Syrians sprinkle it on meats, fish and salads alike to great effect. An electric coffee grinder makes a good processor for hard seeds and grains but ensure it's clean first so as not to taint the flavours.

Barbecues

Noshing *al fresco* – eating and drinking out of doors – is one of our favourite ways of entertaining. In our experience, formality has sometimes got in the way of being able to fully enjoy the event – who hasn't been bored to tears by overly long speeches at weddings? Or complicated food smothered by suspect sauces – outdoor barbecues are the perfect antidote to this.

The food here is usually simply chargrilled (sometimes having been briefly marinated), robustly seasoned and prepared and cooked in full view of the guests.

The Nosh Brothers are not dictatorial when it comes to planning an event, but there are some simple guidelines that will ensure you have a good chance of success.

- Always have plenty of dry charcoal.
- Put plenty of igniter liquid on the charcoal and let it soak in well.
- Then light it, ensuring it's lit properly all over.
- Leave to burn for at least 30 minutes.
- Don't cook anything on it until the coals are grey/white and there is no longer any smell of the lighter fuel to taint the food.
- Ensure the grill is clean and lightly oiled to prevent sticking. The grill should be over a high heat for at least 10 minutes to sterilize it – they are often left in the garage after the last event and rarely cleaned properly.

Barbecuing is one of the few styles of cooking that encourages your guests to be in the kitchen during the cooking. The first thing to remember is you are holding a party without the protection of a roof or walls. This makes for fun, so to get the most out of your party,

1. **NO KIDS**
2. **NO ADULTS WHO BEHAVE LIKE KIDS**
3. **NO TEETOTALLERS**
4. **NO BORES**

With this simple exclusion list you can see it's going to be more fun to start with a hardcore of party people that get a top rating on the high-jinks meter.

Complaints from neighbours are often unavoidable, due to the party happening in the open air. As we normally barbecue in warm weather, your neighbours' windows are usually open too . . . all very obvious! But what do you do when boring old Mr Jones from 7a, next door, shouts over the fence, 'Keep the noise down!'? It's simple, you have several choices. First, if he's not a bad bloke, invite him over. Secondly, if he's a boring old fart, give him a beer and tell him to go away. If he persists, then it should be turned into a sport by throwing things into his garden, like chicken bones, empty beer cans and other such debris. This will get him really mad . . . then you've got a cabaret on your hands . . . free entertainment!

At one time, cooking on wood was the only method of cooking and we've certainly come a long way since then. The new breed of gas barbecues make it possible to maintain a constant cooking temperature for some while, so you can barbecue legs of pork and the like – which previously would have been a bit of a hit-and-miss affair on a charcoal grill, which would have had to be reloaded. Both new-style chargrill and gas barbecues are often provided with a lid either of the flat-cover or rounded 'kettle-lid' type. These also make it possible to contain the heat and smoke and with the addition of dried herbs on the coals or woodchips give the smoky element to the grilling food. With prices ranging from a few pounds for a disposable picked up at a garage on the way to the seaside to £400–£500 for a top-flight gas effort it is worth making the effort to research the model well, before you purchase it – just as you would a car. Unfortunately, you can't test-drive the barbecue so look for the following features:

- Strong construction (moving about and transporting the barbecue puts strain over time on the bolts/joints and welds, etc.).
- Thick, robust gauge of metal used in construction – thin sheets will warp and distort.
- Lid handles made from a non-heat-conducting material (you will be constantly opening the lid to check on progress of cooking).
- A sturdy stand.
- Storage/worktop space attached to the grill assembly. (An area to put or plate-up finished food is useful.)

- If charcoal-fuelled, make sure that there are adjustable slits for ventilation in the bottom 'furnace' part of the grill to allow variable air-flow. This will help you control the heat source.
- The grill bars themselves are not too widely spaced (small items like asparagus may fall through if not orientated across the grill bars properly).

Recipes

Whole duck with soy, anise and orange 57

**Leg of lamb with whole roast onions
and baked potatoes** 58

Lamb kotftes with walnuts and roast chilli dressing 59

**Spatchcocked chicken
with Mesquite barbecue sauce** 60

Italian chicken 62

Serves 4

8 medium or 12 small
    squids, cleaned, heads
    and 'wings' retained
8 tbsp olive oil
1 small onion or 2 shallots
120g minced lean pork
3 large cloves garlic, peeled
2 small red chillies, finely
    chopped
2–3cm piece of ginger root,
    peeled and grated
120g raw peeled prawns
1 tsp tomato purée
1 tbsp fish sauce
4 tbsp chopped fresh
    coriander leaves

To serve
lime wedges
Maldon sea salt

Baby squids stuffed with prawns and pork

This is a winning recipe in the real sense of the word. The *Daily Telegraph* organized a barbecue cook-off between some tele-chefs, including us, with the idea of finding out which country did the best barbecue – Australia, Argentina or South Africa. We Noshes were detailed to represent the Australian corner and we busied ourselves with prawns (of course!), kangaroo fillet and some stuffed squid. Everyone produced great results but the one that clinched the first prize was our stuffed squid. Kathy Lette, the celebrated author, was one of the judges and she praised the general effort, approving that we flew the flag high for Down Under – and we're not even Aussies!

Method

Trim the wings off the squids and chop them small.

Place half the olive oil in a pan and fry the onion or shallots with the pork, garlic, chillies, and ginger for 10 minutes. Add the chopped squid wings and the prawns and sauté for another 2 minutes, then add the tomato purée and fish sauce and season. Add the coriander and stuff the squid cavities with the mixture (not too tightly), securing the flaps closed with soaked wooden toothpicks.

Brush with the remainder of the oil and chargrill for about 5 minutes each on a very hot heat.

Serve with the lime wedges to squeeze and a sprinkling of Maldon sea salt.

Serves 8

½ teacup almond oil
juice of 2 lemons
juice of 2 limes
60g black hand-pitted
    olives,* puréed
freshly ground black
    pepper
8 shark steaks (skin off)
    about 250g each

Shark steaks in almond oil, lemon and olives

Shark is a fish that needs some work, because it can be a little on the bland side. The texture, however, is great and it can be cooked in a number of ways, the skill of a good cook being to pull out the natural flavour in a food and enhance it. A similar dish was cooked for us by a Frenchwoman called Mme Toucane at the back of her boat in St Tropez, and remembering the vast amount of rosé we drank, it was a great afternoon.

Method

Combine all the ingredients except the shark to make a marinade, and immerse the shark in it for at least 1 hour, then grill on a medium to high heat.

* Ensure that if black, they are not factory-pitted. True black olives are well-ripened ones that are too soft in texture to allow easy hand-pitting. The supermarket pitted black olives are frauds. They are green pitted olives that have had a makeover with food colourings to masquerade as black. Avoid them at all costs.

Serves 6

36 langoustines
    (raw or cooked)
240g unsalted butter,
    melted
Maldon sea salt and freshly
    ground black pepper
lemon wedges

Grilled langoustines with lemon and olive oil

Sometimes, if the raw materials are good, the simplest food can be the most satisfying. What could be simpler than langoustines with lemon and olive oil? This is a lunchtime dish (or indeed as a starter for dinner) that we love served with a crisp Italian white wine.

Method

Split the langoustines into halves lengthways, coat with most of the melted butter and season. Place on a solid metal roasting tray or barbecue on a hot grill. If they are already cooked, they will need about 1 minute; if raw, about 2½–3 minutes depending on size. When they're done, brush them again with melted butter and squeeze over them fresh lemon juice. Serve hot. (The shells can be retained for making excellent fish stocks and sauces.)

10 large scallops, cleaned,
the shells cleaned,
scrubbed, dried, and
retained
2 cloves garlic, peeled,
crushed, and chopped
6 tsp chopped parsley
10 tsp olive oil

To serve
lemon wedges

Barbecued scallops on the half shell with garlic, olive oil and parsley

We often get called rich bastards when we cook exotic food like this. Well, we are, but that doesn't stop us sharing these delights with our reader – and by the way, thank you for buying our book and we hope you enjoy it! Plain and simple is often the way and here is a typical example of a delicate dish that's improved by a few traditional seasonings. No need to gild the lily.

Method

Into each empty shell put some garlic and parsley with 1 tsp oil. Grill them on the barbecue for 3 minutes, then place 1 scallop on top of each one. Cover with the kettle lid and cook for 3–5 minutes until the centres are done but not dried out.

Serve immediately, squeezing some fresh lemon juice over.

Whole salmon barbecued in foil with piri-piri spices

Serves 6–8

1 whole salmon, about
    2.25 kg, well scaled,
    washed and cleaned
4 tbsp olive oil
3 tbsp piri-piri spices
Maldon sea salt and freshly
    ground black pepper

No frills or messing about here. Get good-quality fish and grill it plain. Have mayonnaise on the side with green salad and new potatoes if you like but salmon has enough flavour (especially wild salmon if you can get it) to be enjoyed straight up.

Method

Rub the gut cavity and the outside skin of the salmon with olive oil, sprinkle liberally with the piri-piri spices, and season well. Wrap in foil and bake on the grill for 15–25 minutes, with the kettle lid on (if on gas, the heat should be set at maximum), depending on the size of the fish. Very large salmon may take 30 minutes, or more.

Fresh sardines with shaved Parmesan

Serves 3

12 fresh sardines, gutted
    and washed
2 tbsp olive oil
Maldon sea salt and freshly
    ground black pepper

To serve
2 lemons, cut into wedges
120g shaved Parmesan

A world apart from those offerings in a can, fresh sardines have become a fully flavoured and economical way to eat fresh fish. Fine bones preclude much fiddling with the method of cooking – just grill and dress with shaved Parmesan.

Method

Brush the fish with the oil, grill for 5–10 minutes, season, and serve with wedges of lemon and shavings of fresh Parmesan.

Serves 4

2 x 350g fresh monkfish
tails, cleaned and cut
into 24 large dice
360g sliced pancetta
8 x 20cm rosemary stalks
50ml extra virgin oil
50ml lemon juice
freshly ground black
pepper

To serve
½ teacup chopped chives
mixed salad leaves
1 large piece fishskin
cleaned and scaled

Rosemary brochettes of monkfish in pancetta with exotic mixed leaves and fish crackling

Monkfish is firm with no little bones and it won't break up on the barbecue. We like this dish: it looks great on a plate and of course tastes great, the combination of pancetta and rosemary lending a subtle flavour to a superb fish. We like to drink a well-chilled white Burgundy with this.

Monkfish method

Wrap each piece of monkfish in a thin layer of pancetta and make a hole through each one with a skewer. Remove all the leaves from the rosemary stalks, apart from 2cm at the tip, and then push each rosemary stalk through 3 pieces of fish. Lightly drizzle the brochettes with olive oil and the lemon juice and season with freshly ground black pepper.

Cook on a preheated griddle plate or barbecue grill on high, for 2–3 minutes each side but make sure you cover the rosemary leaves with foil to prevent them burning. Serve at once, garnished with the chives.

Mixed leaf salad method

Using fresh ingredients ensures a good result. Red oak-leaf lettuce or batavia is decent although you can get new exotic salad leaves like red chard, shungiko (a dwarf chrysanthemum), mizuna, or the very esoteric types like texel, tatsai, gold or red orach, serrated santo, celtuce and jaba. A little rocket is fine but don't use too much or the taste will dominate the dish. Green salad should be picked clean, washed and drained. It is vital that it is dry (a shake within a clean tea towel will ensure this).

Fish crackling method

English people tend to have an aversion to skin on their fish – perhaps it is a memory of childhood school meals with a soggy grey layer on battered cod looking and tasting like an old flannel. In the Far East, however, crispy skin is a much-prized culinary item and it holds lots of flavour. Like the old favourite, crispy pork crackling from the Sunday roast, it has to be puffed up and really crisp – halfway just won't do. Most skins will cook up well. However, remember, some species of fish like red mullet and sardines have skin that is too delicate to remove without ripping and tearing it. Some, like tuna, will be too tough and thick to cut or cook well so go for an intermediate type, like salmon, mullet, perch, bass or any firm-fleshed 'long' fish – flatfish skin tends to be too sandpapery. A good way to start is to ask your fishmonger (even at your local supermarket) if you can have a salmon skin; make sure it is scaled and wash it down for good measure. Drain and dry it thoroughly and pat dry with a clean tea towel. Deep-fry it in hot oil (180°C/350°F), either whole and served as a large piece to be broken up with a fork, or (we think the better way) cut into very thin 'julienne' slices and cooked in batches until crisp.

Barbecued red snapper with basil and lemon

3 whole red snappers

Maldon sea salt and freshly ground white pepper

3 large basil leaves

1 lemon, cut into thirds lengthways

8 tbsp olive oil

juice of 3 lemons

We've all seen those wire grilling frames in the shape of a fish (or several sardine-sized forms). They usually end up covered in dust at the back of the garage. So dust yours off and season it – brush it with oil and allow the oil to be burnt off on the barbecue grill (using the hot-kettle lid). This will prevent the fish skin sticking and peeling off.

Method

The snappers should be gutted and washed clean (ask your fish-monger to do this if you're squeamish) and the scales removed with the back of a kitchen knife. Cut three diagonal slashes in the main body of the flesh on each side, trim off the gill fins and season the cavities.

Wrap a basil leaf round each piece of lemon and place them in the cavities of the snappers. Brush the fish with the oil and place them in the wire frame. Grill for about 8–10 minutes each side depending on size, sprinkle the lemon juice over, season, and serve.

Tuna in orange and chilli marinade

4 large yellowfin fresh tuna
    steaks (about 1–2cm
    thick)

Marinade
juice of 4 oranges
a large handful of chopped
    coriander leaves
1 tbsp red chilli paste
6 tbsp olive oil
2 cloves garlic, peeled and
    chopped
1 mild onion
Maldon sea salt

You will need
250g woodchips

Originally a Tex-Mex combination, we have adapted this absolutely foolproof recipe for any combination of Mediterranean-style themes. So long as you prepare it from the very freshest fish and let it marinate a decent time it's hard to go wrong. A stunningly simple combination.

Method

Blend all the marinade ingredients until smooth and rest the tuna in it for about 1 hour. Meanwhile soak the woodchips in warm water and drain.

Preheat the grill to maximum if gas or until the charcoals are white and very hot. Scatter a handful of damp chips over the coals until the chips are smoking then cover with the kettle lid and then grill the tuna about 15cm above the coals, for about 4 minutes each side, basting with the marinade once when turning the steaks over and seasoning.

When ready, the fish should be brown outside and have a pink centre.

Tuna in orange and chilli marinade

Serves 3 or 1 Nosh

New York chilli dogs with cheese

Nosh chilli

3 tbsp olive oil

2 medium onions, chopped

2 chopped bell peppers
(1 red, 1 green)

2 crushed cloves garlic

950g coarsely chopped or
minced beef (skirt is
good)

1 x 360g can chopped
tomatoes

1 tube or small jar tomato
purée

2 pickled jalapeño peppers,
rinsed, seeded, and
chopped (El Paso brand
is good)

1½ tbsp chilli powder

1 tsp paprika

½ tsp Maldon sea salt

1 tsp oregano

2 tsp ground cumin

1 x 360g can pinto beans,
drained

To serve

3 large smoked frankfurters

3 long white rolls

300ml NOSH CHILLI

Gruyère or raclette cheese

a selection of exotic
mustards

I think this is why brother Mick is so large. Once he starts on the old chilli dogs, that's it – there's no stopping him. Although the quantities below are for three, Mick regards three as a single Nosh portion and always goes back for seconds. It is common for people to use red kidney beans for chillies but we feel they are rather indigestible and if used as a topping render the dish heavy, so we recommend pinto beans – the traditional Tex-Mex alternative.

Chilli method

In a large heavy cast-iron pan or casserole heat the oil and fry the onions with the peppers and garlic until the onions are soft, then add the meat and brown it (about 5 minutes). Add all remaining ingredients except the beans and simmer the chilli for 1–1½ hours until the meat is tender, stirring frequently to prevent sticking. Adjust the liquid towards the end if the mixture gets too dry. (It should be moist but not runny.)

Add the beans and cook for another 30 minutes.

Hot dog method

Grill the hot dog, and heat a bun. Split the bun, add the chilli dog, spoon on a generous amount of Nosh chilli and top with grated Gruyère or raclette cheese. Place the dog back on the grill in a metal tray and replace the kettle lid for a few minutes to melt the cheese. Add mustard and serve.

Serves 4

a small bunch of spring
onions (including flags)
3–4 tbsp sour cream
4 pickled jalapeño peppers,
chopped
950g coarse-ground
(medium-fat) beef skirt
Maldon sea salt and freshly
ground black pepper

To serve
fresh white seeded
hamburger rolls

Hamburgers with sour cream and jalapeños

We all like hamburgers, but once people get them onto a barbecue all the wheels seem to drop off and we end up with carbon patties or chunks that haven't fallen through the grill bars. Shun supermarket mince, which is basically offcuts of meat mulched to a dog-food under some clingfilm, and use decent beef skirt, freshly minced from your local butcher, to order. No need for egg to bind, just a dollop of sour cream and jalapeños for a real Tex-Mex taste.

Method

Chop the spring onions finely, and combine with the sour cream, jalapeños, and beef, and season. Don't overdo the cream or the mix will be sloppy: add just enough to bind the meat. Shape into patties about 10 cm across and 2cm thick and grill on a medium to hot grill for about 5–7 minutes each side to achieve a well-done outside with a moist, pink centre. Season and serve in the hamburger rolls.

For 12 large pork ribs

300ml tomato ketchup
1 tsp Chinese five-spice
    powder
juice of 3 lemons
juice of 3 oranges
3 tbsp brown sugar
4 tbsp honey
5 tbsp dark soy sauce
3 cloves garlic, crushed
8 cm piece of fresh root
    ginger, finely grated
2 star anise

Barbecued Chinese-style ribs – the ultimate recipe

This is by far the best way to eat ribs. It's economical to buy and easy too because most of the cooking can be done in the oven; just chargrill them quickly on the barbecue grill when you want to serve them. This will caramelize the sweet sauce, and these are the tenderest and most succulent of all the ribs we've ever tasted.

Allow 6 large ribs or 12 small per person for a main dish. If the dish is part of a meal with a varied selection you can reduce the ribs to 3 large or 6 small per person.

Method

Combine all the ingredients and coat the ribs well. There's no need to add salt as the soy will provide enough. Pile the ribs into a high-sided oven roasting dish and cover with foil. Roast for 1½ hours in a preheated oven (150°C/300°F/gas mark 2), turning the ribs at least once, and basting them well. When the meat is soft (you can see this by the meaty part of the rib shrinking away from the bone slightly), place the tray on the hob top over a high flame and boil the sauce to reduce it to a sticky consistency – enough to coat the ribs. Then they are ready for the barbecue. (Place in tightly lidded plastic containers if you're transporting them far.) Then, simply finish off on a high heat part of the grill to caramelize the sauce and serve warm with any spare sauce for dipping into.

Summer Nosh

6 wings

2 tbsp peanut oil

3 tbsp lime juice (juice of
about 3 limes)

2 tbsp Thai fish sauce

½ small red chilli, deseeded
and finely chopped

12 basil leaves, chopped

Maldon sea salt

Chicken wings in Thai basil, lime and fish sauce

We own up to having stolen this boning idea from a chef who cooks on TV, but like all things we've stolen we have developed it – or as we say, Noshed it up a bit. Wings are the most economical cut of chicken and you can't eat cheaper than this, unless you do a runner from a restaurant.

Method

Remove the 'winglet' end of the wing and discard it. Cut across the small knuckle joint to expose the two wing bones and push the flesh down to the other end, turning it inside out (like an umbrella). Push out and discard the smaller of the two wing bones, and pull the meat right out into an umbrella shape, so that the remaining bone acts as a handle that can be discarded after eating. Combine all the ingredients except the salt and rest the chicken pieces in the marinade, meat side down, for at least 1 hour. Then salt the chicken and grill it on a medium-hot part of the barbecue for about 10–15 minutes to cook thoroughly. Baste with remaining liquor just before the end. Serve with the bones to view, upright.

Serves 6

Classic Tandoori chicken

3 tbsp sour-type yogurt
juice of 3 lemons
a pinch of Maldon sea salt
2 tbsp olive oil
4 tbsp Tandoori paste
6 chicken breasts (at least
180g each), skinned and
diced into 3–4 pieces
for skewering

This works very well cold, so if you're off to the seaside for the day, pack some in some foil for the trip (if the traffic is bad it makes a nice snack in the car). A little salad can be served (with lemon juice dressing), and some pitta bread goes well. To drink? Ice-cold lager is good (but don't let the driver have any – no matter how much he or she pleads!).

Method

The chicken used for Tandoori in Indian restaurants is usually second-grade meat, so premier-quality chicken will heighten the quality of the dish.

Blend all the other ingredients into a thick paste and smear all over the diced chicken, mixing well with your hands to ensure even coating. Leave for at least 1 hour (3–4 is better) and then skewer them, season fully with salt and grill on the hottest heat for about 3 minutes each side, turning over to cook evenly. Season with extra salt while on the grill.

The marinade will tend to burn in 'hot spots' – this is OK and will give a sort of authentic Tandoori feel to the dish.

Serves 4

1 whole duck, cleaned, split
  along the backbone and
  hinged open
3 cloves garlic, crushed
juice of 4 oranges
zest of 1 orange
8 tbsp soy sauce
3 tbsp ground aniseed
  powder
1 tbsp soft brown sugar
4 tbsp peanut oil

Whole duck with soy, anise and orange

Delish – that's all I can think of for this intro. Suffice to say, it's loads better than that poncy old French nonsense, Duck à l'Orange.

Method

Prick the duck skin all over with a sharp fork. Mix all the other ingredients together and marinate the duck for at least 1 hour. There should be no need for additional salt on this as we have specified a good quantity of soy, which is quite salty enough.

Grill bone-side down for about 40 minutes on a medium heat, checking to ensure even cooking without burning. For barbecuing this dish you'll need to use the kettle lid (if you have one). Flip over to finish the skin side for about 15 minutes or until cooked crispy, basting with the marinade, taking care not to burn the skin.

Serves 2–3

Leg of lamb with whole roast onions and baked potatoes

1.8 kg leg of lamb, ankle
   bone removed
4 large cloves garlic, peeled
   and sliced lengthways
   into 3
a small bunch of fresh
   rosemary
75g butter, softened
freshly ground black
   pepper
3 medium onions
   (whole, skin on)
3 medium red onions
   (whole, skin on)
6 whole baking potatoes

To serve
CLASSIC VINAIGRETTE
   (page 170)
Maldon sea salt
freshly ground black
   pepper
300ml sour cream
240g salted butter (Jersey
   butter is good)
a small bunch of chives,
   chopped

To barbecue a whole leg of lamb is eaier than you might imagine. You will need a barbecue with a kettle lid as the cooking time needs to be slower than normal. If you're using charcoal you will need a well-ignited deep layer. Do not attempt it with a shallow layer – it burns too hot at first and not for long enough to cook a large piece of meat.

April normally sees the new season's lamb in the shops and this is a perfect dish to try it out on.

Method
Preheat the grill to full heat. With a small sharp knife, make about 12 incisions in the lamb, 5cm deep in the fleshy side of the joint. Insert a piece of garlic and a small sprig of rosemary into each one, pushing all of them right in with your little finger. Cream the butter and smear it all over the surface of the meat. Grind plenty of black pepper over it, and place it on the hottest part of the grill.

Roast the lamb for 1½ hours or so, rotating the joint every so often, depending on the size of the joint and how well done you like your meat, then take it out and leave it to rest in a warm place, covered with foil, for 15 minutes before carving. Because it's grilled there is no possibility of serving the meat with any juices or gravy so try the classic vinaigrette.

The onions can be baked whole with their skins on in a foil tray stacked together for about 1 hour or more. To serve them, prise open the top of each onion with a sharp paring knife and insert a little butter. The potatoes will take about 1–1½ hours. Wrap them in foil for the first half-hour and then uncover them to crisp up. Serve split with plenty of salt and pepper, sour cream, butter and chives.

Serves 4

720g best lamb mince
   (lean leg)
3 ripe red peppers, skinned,
   cored, deseeded, and
   finely diced
1 tsp ground cinnamon
1 tsp ground coriander seed
1 tsp ground cumin
2 shallots, finely chopped
4 tbsp finely chopped
   coriander leaf
120g finely chopped shelled
   walnuts (use pine nuts
   if you're allergic)
virgin olive oil
Maldon sea salt and freshly
   ground black pepper

Lamb kotftes with walnuts and roast chilli dressing

Ottoman food is such a delight if done properly. The use of spices has to be balanced and of course, they have to be fresh. The problem with old spices is that if the aromatic quality so important to the dish goes, the dish is 'dead'. So often, we've seen people jabbing dried powdered spice with the back of a teaspoon to scrape a bit out of a jar that's probably 10 years old. Bad news – don't do it.

Method

Mince the meat and all the other ingredients except the oil, salt and pepper in a food processor on fast until smooth textured, then season. Shape it into long flattish sausages and arrange on flat metal skewers. Brush with oil and grill on a low to medium heat for about 5 minutes each side. Serve seasoned in warmed pitta breads, with some salad and a spoonful of roast chilli dressing.

Roast chilli dressing

4 red peppers
3 fresh red chillies
1 tbsp vinegar
juice of 1 lemon
6 tbsp olive oil
Maldon sea salt and freshly
   ground black pepper

Method

Roast the red peppers and chillies over a flame or in a preheated oven (250°C/475°F/gas mark 9) to blister the skins, then place them in a bowl and sweat them under clingfilm until cool enough to touch. Peel the skins off, deseed and core them, and process on high speed with the vinegar, lemon juice and oil, then season.

Spatchcocked chicken with Mesquite barbecue sauce

8 chicken quarters, on the
    bone, skin on

Marinade
juice of 10 limes
4 measures tequila
10 tbsp olive oil
juice of 4 oranges
3 cloves garlic, peeled and
    crushed
1 tsp mild chilli powder
4 tbsp liquid Mesquite
    smoke*
Maldon sea salt and freshly
    ground black pepper

To serve
MESQUITE BARBECUE
    SAUCE

This recipe is the perfect antidote to battery-farmed chickens with no particular flavour; the Tex-Mex seasonings and the potent warlock barbecue sauce combine to make a dull bird something to look forward to. If your budget stretches to premier-quality free-range or corn-fed birds, you won't regret spending the extra: this recipe transforms top-quality birds into a sublime taste experience. When asked once what the best way to prepare a Southern chicken dish was, Nick replied, 'Get your slave to do it for you.' Mick cheerily informed him that slavery had been abolished in Britain some hundreds of years before. Nick's retort? 'Can we bring it back?' When informed that this was an unlikely event he consoled himself with the rich barbecue sauce. It's a taste of the Lone Star state.

Method

Slash each chicken piece a couple of times across the skin. Mix the marinade ingredients together well and marinate the chicken for 2 hours, turning the pieces occasionally.

    Grill them well for 30–40 minutes, slowly basting them with the marinade and ensuring that any spits of flame flaring up from the barbecue are doused immediately. Cover with the barbecue sauce and serve warm.

Mesquite barbecue sauce

3 tbsp olive oil

1 Spanish onion, peeled
and chopped

2 cloves garlic, peeled and
crushed

1 tbsp mild chilli powder

½ tsp Chinese five-spice
powder

1 x 360g can Italian peeled
plum tomatoes, pulped

1 red pepper, peeled and
chopped

1 bottle Dos Equis beer

2 tbsp honey

150ml tomato ketchup

3 tbsp soft brown sugar

2cm piece of ginger root,
peeled and grated

2 tbsp cider vinegar

1 tbsp black treacle

1 tsp soy sauce

½ tsp liquid mesquite
smoke*

Method

In a heavy-based saucepan, heat the oil and sauté the onion and garlic slowly until soft (about 15 minutes, covered), then stir in the chilli powder and five-spice powder and cook on for another few minutes.

Stir in the tomatoes, red pepper, Dos Equis, honey, tomato ketchup, sugar, ginger, vinegar, treacle, soy sauce, and liquid smoke and simmer for 30 minutes until the sauce has thickened and is shiny. Cool the sauce for serving.

With a kettle-lid barbecue it is an easy matter to create smoke by smouldering woodchips or damp herbs over the coals. With a gas barbecue it is somewhat harder to create smoke so we recommend the use of Liquid Smoke. You may have seen these small American imports labelled Hickory or Mesquite Smoke. They are very concentrated essences and you only need add a little to a marinade. For a light smoke flavour a few drops brushed on with some oil is sufficient; a heavier impression is easily imparted by allowing the food to rest in the essence for an hour or two.

Italian chicken

4 boned chicken breasts
(at least 180g each)

Marinade
6 tbsp olive oil
6 cloves garlic, coarsely
chopped
juice and sliced skin of
4 lemons
4 large sprigs rosemary
freshly ground black
pepper

We have had magnificent success with this dish. It's foolproof! A while ago, we organized a wedding for some close friends, Tracey and Jo. (Tracey was the groom, by the way.) They had over 500 guests and one of the dishes we prepared was this Italian chicken. This classic way of preparing the chicken is so good because so often breast meat dries out on a barbecue and becomes unpalatable as a result. Marinating takes care of this problem. At the time of going to press Tracey and Jo are still married and what's more still talking to us.

Method

Make 3 deepish slashes in the top surface of each chicken breast and discard the skin. Combine the marinade ingredients and marinate the breasts for at least two hours.

If you're presenting the chicken on skewers, dice it into 2 cm chunks; immerse wooden skewers in warm water to prevent them burning.

Five minutes' grilling is usually enough. If any lemon peel adheres to the meat, don't worry. Once grilled, it is perfectly edible – and delicious too.

On the Patio

In the world of commercial food preparation, 'light' foods often means 'low-flavour'. Many people equate 'low-fat' with desirable produce and the advertising agencies conspire to help propel this image forward. To us it smacks of brainwashing. British food-lovers have become over-enamoured in their love affair, for crème fraiche instead of real cream, yogurt instead of real mayonnaise and margarines instead of butter.

Lightness can be achieved in a variety of ways, including innately lighter textures (e.g. cooking fish in summer and the heavier game meats in autumn and winter), flavoured oils rather than heavy sauces, fruit coulis as a dressing, etc., so that lightness of effect is achieved with items of real value that enhance the dish rather than by substituting out of paranoia a copycat ingredient that doesn't have the full complement of tastes.

Recipes

Ciabatta

450g strong plain flour
2 tsp Maldon sea salt
1 sachet easy-blend dried
    yeast*
250ml hand-warm water
4 tbsp virgin olive oil
Maldon sea salt and freshly
    ground black pepper

Ciabatta is an olive oil bread from Italy, the recipe for which can easily be adapted to carry any one or more of a variety of herbs or cheeses to flavour it. The unique detail of ciabatta is that the dough, once risen, is not knocked back into a smooth close texture but is left open to give a crisp crust with large holes which give the loaf a rustic feel.

Method

Sift the flour into a warm mixing bowl, make a well in the centre, and add the salt and yeast. Pour in the water and the olive oil, drawing in the flour gradually, and knead the dough until smooth and elastic for 5 minutes. Place in the floured bowl, cover with clingfilm, and put the bowl in a warm place for 1 hour, or until the dough has doubled in size. Then shape the ciabatta dough ('ciabatta' is literally 'slipper') into a flat oval and season lightly with salt and pepper.

Fold the dough over to make a loaf shape and place on a floured baking tray. Paint the top of the loaf dough with virgin olive oil and sprinkle with some more salt, then bake in a preheated oven (220°C/425°F/gas mark 7) oven for 25–30 minutes depending on the thickness of the dough.

Allow to cool slightly before cutting, but this bread is best served warm. If reheating from cold, warm for 10 minutes or so at 140°C/275°F/gas mark 1) oven before serving.

Modern active dried yeasts mean that we can mix the yeast powder directly into the flour mix these days without having to make a 'starter' mix, which saves time. If you feel like being a purist, there is nothing wrong with using fresh yeast, which is easily obtainable from any good health food store's refrigerated section. But we reckon the new dried active stuff is fine.

Serves 4

8 corn tortillas
unsalted butter for frying
16 small eggs*
Maldon sea salt and freshly
    ground black pepper

To serve
575ml RANCHERO SAUCE
250g grated Gruyère cheese
    (Monterey Jack is
    traditional, if a little
    bland)
slices of firm, ripe avocado

Huevos Rancheros: eggs, tortillas and ranchero sauce

This is a particular favourite of a friend of ours, Julie Roach, and we look forward to the concept of a spicy start to the day after she converted us. It's not the sort of breakfast to eat every day, but is perfect for a late brunch on a Sunday, or if you have a hangover and want to give your brain something else to worry about!

You should find it easy to get reasonable tortillas from your supermarket. Making them from scratch to a proper formula is almost impossible in Europe because they are made from nixtamal, which requires a long process of cooking up white corn with lime until dry – so buy yours ready-made.

Huevos rancheros – 'ranch-style eggs' – are traditionally served as fried eggs on a floury tortilla bread with a spicy tomato sauce on top and a few slices of firm, ripe avocado to decorate. The sauce is simple and easy; make it in a larger quantity and it will keep in plastic, covered in the fridge, for up to 1 week.

Method

Grill the tortillas and keep them warm under a cloth. Heat the butter and fry the eggs gently on a low heat, then season them and place them on the tortillas. Smother with a generous amount of the warm sauce, scatter with grated Gruyère cheese and lay some slices of avocado on top.

* Use free-range eggs wherever possible. They cost more than battery eggs but do give better taste results when used in a dish alone. Small eggs come from younger birds and also give better results.

Ranchero sauce

1 medium onion, very
    finely chopped
1 tbsp olive oil
1 clove garlic, pulped
2 pickled jalapeños, finely
    chopped
150ml chicken stock
150ml TOMATO AND BASIL
    SAUCE
a pinch of oregano
Maldon sea salt and freshly
    ground black pepper

Method

Sauté the onion lightly in the oil until soft on a medium flame and add the garlic. Then add the jalapeños, stock, tomato and basil sauce, and oregano. Bring to the boil and then simmer for 5 minutes, until all the elements blend together. Remove from the heat and season to taste then keep the sauce warm until needed.

* Remember, as the tomato sauce reduces in volume, the degree of saltiness does too, so don't adjust the final seasoning until the end of the reduction process.

Tomato and basil sauce

6 x 400g tins of Italian
    plum tomatoes
175ml good olive oil
1 large Spanish onion,
    peeled and finely
    chopped
6 large whole cloves garlic
1 large bunch of basil
    (including stalks)
3 tbsp oregano
1 tbsp caster sugar
2 tsp Maldon sea salt
½ tsp ground white pepper
60g unsalted butter

Method

Pass the tomatoes through a mouli sieve (fine grade) to remove seeds and skin. This is most important. The skins and seeds are not digestible and do not add anything to the flavour. Heat the olive oil in a solid-based saucepan over a medium heat and add the onion, garlic, basil and oregano.

Stir briskly to prevent the onion browning; when it has softened, add the tomato pulp. Bring the mixture to the boil and immediately reduce the heat to a low simmer.

Stir in the sugar (this balances the acidity of the tomatoes) and half of the salt.

Simmer the sauce for about 30 minutes until well-reduced. The solids will tend to condense on the bottom of the pan, so stir with a wooden spoon occasionally. The time taken for this process will vary depending on the degree of wateriness of the original tinned tomato contents, so keep an eye on it.

When the sauce is finished it should be tested for seasoning (add ground white pepper, and the butter to give it a good 'shine') and that it has a rich, thick texture.

On the Patio

Potato rösti with poached eggs, smoked salmon and stir-fried spinach

Rösti

675g potatoes, peeled and
  finely grated

1 tsp fine table salt

1 Spanish onion, peeled
  and finely grated

½ tsp Maldon sea salt

5 small eggs, lightly beaten

6 tbsp dry white
  breadcrumbs

freshly ground black
  pepper

oil for frying (sunflower,
  corn, and peanut are
  good)

Poached eggs

8 eggs

white wine vinegar

Salmon and spinach

4 handfuls of washed baby
  spinach

a small knob of unsalted
  butter

sea salt

a pinch of ground nutmeg

4 large slices of smoked
  salmon

We are indebted to Gerry D'Angelo for many fine breakfasts in The Sports Bard in Sydney and this is typical of a brunch dish on the menu. Stolen unashamedly, we reproduce it here for you to get a flavour of life Down Under. Close your eyes and you might just about hear the surf in Bondi.

Rösti method

Sprinkle the potato with the table salt. Mix and squeeze the potato against the side of a wire sieve, letting the juices drain out. Discard the juices. Stir the onion, the sea salt, and the eggs into the potato and mix together. It will be a little sloppy so add some breadcrumbs to soak up and stiffen the mix. Season with pepper. Divide the mixture into rösti about 10 cm across and 1 cm thick.

Heat some oil in a large heavy-based pan on a medium flame and shallow-fry the rösti, flattening each pancake with the back of a spoon, until crisp and brown on both sides. Try not to cook these too quickly or the centre of the rösti will be raw-tasting and crunchy with the outside burnt. Try a couple for 3–4 minutes each side and adjust the time according to your stove heat. It is also important to have the oil at the right temperature: too hot, and the rösti will be raw inside and over-brown on the edges; too cool, and they will tend to absorb the oil and become soggy and inedible.

Poached eggs method

Use free-range eggs wherever possible. They cost more than battery eggs but do give better results when used in a dish alone. Small eggs come from younger birds and also give better results.

You might think it's flogging a dead horse to mention how to poach eggs but it's amazing how many people have asked us the best way to get good results. Our preferred method is to ignore those patent shallow-dish poachers that come with a grid and steamer-lid and go for the old-fashioned tried-and-tested way, i.e. break one single egg at a time into just boiling water with a small dash of white wine vinegar.

The water must not be boiling too violently or the whites will be spread around the pan in watery flakes. The vinegar helps to set the eggs quickly but don't add too much or the egg will have an over-powering sour taste. A quick swirl of a dessert or serving spoon to create a 'whirlpool' in the middle of the saucepan just before you add the egg will also help to quickly spin and firm the egg whites neatly around the yolk and form an attractive oval that would not look out of place at The Savoy. Cracking the egg into a teacup first before adding helps ensure that you don't add broken-yolked eggs to the pan. Fishing out with a slotted spoon should then be easy and although personal preferences vary, leave at least 2–3 minutes before attempting to remove the egg – otherwise it will be too runny to pick up. Watch the timing closely to prevent hard yolks.

Salmon and spinach method and assembly
Wok some baby spinach with a little butter, some salt and ground nutmeg, drain the juices and wrap the drained spinach in smoked salmon: place on the poached eggs over the large rösti.

Antipasto risotto

Risotto

100g unsalted butter

4 tbsp virgin olive oil

1 Spanish onion, peeled
and finely chopped

600g Arborio rice

2 cloves garlic, crushed and
minced

300ml white wine

3 tbsp chopped basil leaves

2 bay leaves

1.3 litres chicken stock, hot

8 black olives

6 cloves roasted garlic,
skinned

6 MOON-DRIED TOMATOES

Maldon sea salt

100g pecorino cheese,
coarsely grated

freshly ground black
pepper

Antipasto

8 thin slices Serrano or
Parma ham

4 slices Galia melon

4 baby aubergines,
seasoned, halved, and
chargrilled

4 MOON-DRIED TOMATOES

12 chilli and garlic-
marinated olives

120g bufala mozzarella,
cut into wedges

extra-virgin olive oil

Risotto is to the nineties what mashed potato was to the eighties: the perfect medium to carry simple flavours easily and cheaply. With only moderate skill, most cooks could execute a reasonable effort. Here it's simply the centrepiece of a traditional Italian antipasto platter.

Risotto method

In a heavy-based saucepan on a medium-low flame, melt the butter with the olive oil and add the onion. Cook slowly, turning frequently, until the onion becomes transparent. Add the rice and crushed garlic and heat for another 2–3 minutes, turning constantly to seal the rice. Add the wine and the herbs, and stir. Add half the stock, and the olives, roasted garlic, and tomatoes and stir constantly. The liquid will reduce as the rice cooks, so each time the rice becomes dry add a little hot stock to keep the risotto 'flowing'. The consistency you want is moist, not soupy; the rice is cooked *al dente*. Just before serving, check the seasoning, then add the pecorino cheese and freshly ground black pepper.

Assembly

Spoon a generous ladle of risotto onto the centre of the plate, arrange the antipasto items around the edge, and pour a light swirl of top-quality extra-virgin olive oil over.

Moon-dried tomatoes

We call these 'moon-dried tomatoes' in deference to the outdoor 'sun-dried' Italian imports. You can make these easily in your own home . . . while you sleep . . . literally!

Method

You must have the plum type of Italian tomatoes. It doesn't matter if they are a bit overripe or bruised, in fact this recipe is perfect for tomatoes that are a bit squishy or 'over' for fresh salads.

Wash the tomatoes and dry them. Next, cut horizontally along the long centre line of the tomato (bisecting it from stem point north to south). If the stem end has a very white hard pith core, remove it with a sharp paring knife and discard it. Arrange the tomato halves cut side up on a wire cake rack (on a flat baking tray they will burn). Brush each cut surface with olive oil and season with sea salt and a twist of freshly ground black pepper.

Bake overnight in a very, very low oven (50°C/125°F/the very lowest gas) until they have dried out and shrivelled somewhat. In Italy the tradition is to remove the seeds and core, which gives a dryish, chewy result; with the watery core left in, there is a moister feel on the palate. This is a dish that can be made after you have baked something in the oven on a high heat. All you have to do is to switch the oven off, place the racks of tomatoes inside and shut the door. The natural decrease in temperature will accommodate the process needed for best results. If you have an Aga solid-top-type oven, the plate-warming cupboard section is best for this. You may need to keep the tomatoes in for 24 hours! Keep an eye on them. Slow and even is the way.

The tomatoes can be preserved in a Kilner jar of good quality olive oil. The oil itself can even be flavoured with garlic and herbs such as thyme to vary the results. So long as the dried tomatoes are covered they will not become mildewed. They will keep for a couple of months in a cold place and about six in a cold fridge. The oil will solidify so thaw it out if you just want to remove a couple of tomatoes for a single dish.

On the Patio

Serves 6

12 slices CIABATTA
    (page 65)
1 tsp virgin olive oil
Maldon sea salt
50g small pine nuts
    (Lebanese are best)
60g unsalted butter
180g Gorgonzola*
60g full-fat cream cheese
1 tbsp chopped flat-leaf
    parsley
1 tbsp finely chopped
    chives
freshly ground black
    pepper

Gorgonzola and toasted pine nut crostinis

Strong flavours and textures make for a pile of appetizers that if you're not careful will leave no room for the main – they're that good!

Method

Cut 1cm slices of ciabatta, brush with the olive oil, sprinkle with salt, and bake in a preheated oven (200°C/400°F/gas mark 6) for a few minutes until golden brown. Toast the pine nuts lightly in a dry frying pan until a light gold colour. Mix together the butter, Gorgonzola, and cream cheese, sprinkling in the parsley and chives. Season to taste, spread on the ciabatta, and top with the pine nuts.

* If you cannot get Gorgonzola, a good, ripe Dolcelatte makes a suitable, if slightly milder, substitute, that really is decent. (This has also been done with great effect using Ireland's famous Cashel Blue.)

Capsicum and aubergine roulade

It's rare to get a Nosh recipe into one of our books that has no meat in it but this one has quite a degree of class and sophistication. Looks pretty on the plate too! Take care to sprinkle only the finest of olive oils at the end.

Serves 8

8 large red bell peppers
300ml olive oil
6 small aubergines
Maldon sea salt and freshly
    ground black pepper
a bunch of long green
    chives, uncut

To serve
3 tbsp finely chopped
    flat-leaf parsley
100ml extra-virgin olive oil

Method

Preheat the oven to the maximum temperature. (If the oven is set too low, the peppers will over-roast and become fragile and difficult to handle for the roulade.) Coat the peppers with 2 tbsp of the olive oil and blister them in the oven for about 10–15 minutes. Remove them, place them on a cool tray, and cover them with clingfilm for about 15–20 minutes, which will help the skin slide off as they sweat and cool. Cut lengthways to open them up flat, skin them, and discard the seeds.

Slice the aubergines lengthways into 1cm strips and salt well to draw out any bitter juices. Let them stand for 30 minutes, then wash the slices in cold running water, drain and then wipe dry with a tea-towel.

In a large frying pan heat the remaining olive oil (not the virgin stuff for dressing) over a medium-hot flame and fry the slices of aubergine until golden on both sides (for 4–6 minutes or so). Drain on kitchen paper. When all the aubergines have been fried, allow them to cool.

On a smooth-topped work surface spread a long sheet of clingfilm. Arrange flattened 'sheets' of peppers side by side in a rectangle without leaving any spaces between them. Next, arrange a layer of aubergines on top, again, leaving no gaps. Season with salt and pepper and lay the chives in a sheet along the length of the roll. Using the edge of the plastic to gather together the roulade, start to roll up the length of the top edge and draw it tight towards you. Tuck the leading edge under, applying some firm degree of pressure to get a nice cylinder of roulade. Now twist the ends like a sweetie wrapper to shape up a nice cylindrical tube and tie off the ends with a bag twist or string then chill in the coldest part of your fridge for 1 hour.

To serve, unwrap when well chilled and slice across the grain in 1cm-thick slices. Arrange on the plate in neat discs and sprinkle with black pepper, a pinch of Maldon sea salt with the parsley and pour over the extra-virgin olive oil.

Capsicum and aubergine roulade

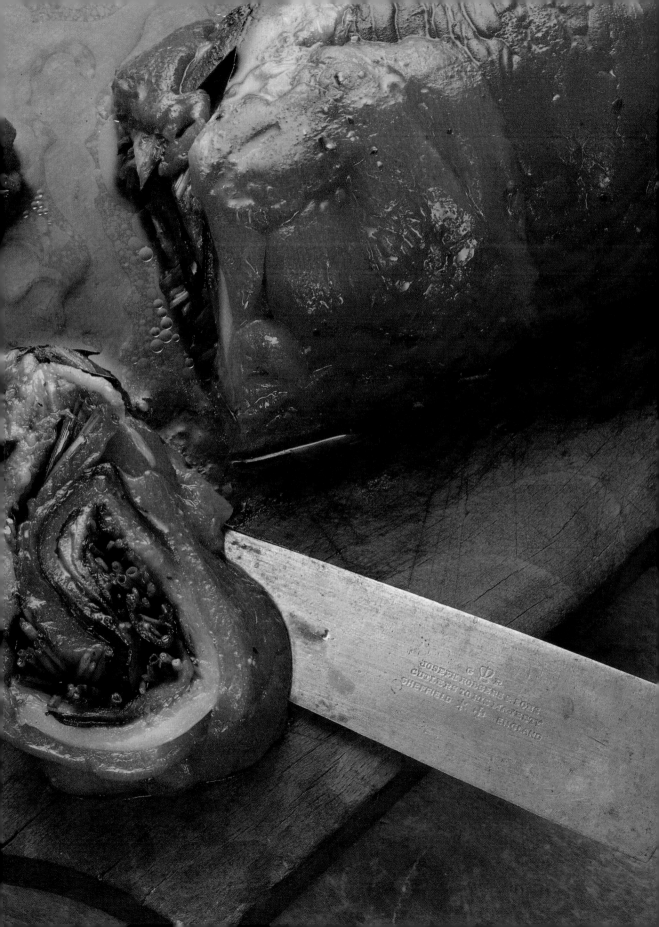

Serves 6

90g unsalted butter

1 tbsp virgin olive oil

1 tbsp caster sugar

2 red peppers, cored, cut
into 6 pieces

4 small red onions, cut into
quarters and blanched

12 large spring onions

2 ripe, tasty courgettes, cut
into thick diagonal
slices

2 green peppers, cored and
cut into 6 pieces

12 small hard cherry
tomatoes

12 small button onions
or 'banana' shallots,
roasted for 10 minutes

12 asparagus spears,
blanched

12 sugar snap peas

12 baby sweetcorns,
blanched and halved

Maldon sea salt and freshly
ground black pepper

400g fresh puff pastry

Tarte Tatin of summer vegetables with beetroot sauce

Why not vegetables? It works fine with fruits, so . . . ? Just remember, the vegetables are being cooked all together at the same time, so prepare each one by cutting, arranging, or blanching it (or any combination) so that they are all perfectly cooked at the end. Beetroots are much underused by the domestic cook and we advise you to think again about these hard-working roots!

Tart method

Preheat the oven to 250°C/475°F/gas mark 9.

Place the butter and oil in a heavy-based cast iron or mild steel frying pan with a metal handle (no wood or plastic as the tart is going into the oven itself in the frying pan) over a high flame and melt the butter (taking care not to burn it). Add the sugar and stir it around to dissolve it. Off the heat, arrange the vegetables neatly, remembering that when the tart is cooked, the side you will see is the layer at the bottom of the pan. Use the smaller vegetables to fill in the gaps. Season the layer of vegetables.

Return to the heat and allow the butter/sugar mix to caramelize and colour up the vegetable surfaces, then turn the flame down to medium. Ensure they do not burn unduly (although some crisping up of the peppers' skin will give flavour and texture). The smell of the sugar turning to caramel will have a distinctive aroma – when the tart vegetables have cooked through (about 5 minutes should do it) you must turn off the heat, remove the pan to a wooden board nearby and place over it a rolled disc of the puff pastry 3 mm thick, leaving a 4 cm overlap that can be tucked down under the bottom edge with the handle of a dessert spoon (this will be the sides of the tart when inverted). Using a spoon will help prevent the sides tearing.

Now place the pan, complete with pastry lid, in the middle of the oven for 10–15 minutes to allow the puff pastry to bake and rise up. When ready, remove the pan using heavy oven cloths (remember, the metal handle is red-hot!). The pastry will tend to subside a little on cooling – don't worry. Slide the blade of a knife around the edges to ensure there's no sticking to the pan.

Place a large flat dinner plate on top of the pan and flip the pan neatly over. Tap the bottom with the handle of a wooden spoon to check the layer has dropped evenly. When you remove the pan the layer should have turned out neatly. Don't panic if there are rogue bits of veg sticking to the pan bottom, simply flick them out with a knife and glue them back in the place from which they escaped.

To serve, cut into wedges and spoon some beetroot sauce around them.

Beetroot sauce

3 small cooked whole
    beetroots, diced small
300ml single cream
Maldon sea salt and freshly
    ground black pepper
juice of ½ a lemon
1 tsp hot horseradish sauce

Method

Heat the beetroots with the cream in a small saucepan. Season, add the lemon juice and horseradish and blitz with a blender or soup whizzer and check seasoning again. The consistency should be about that of thick single cream, robust but not stiff – you should just be able to pour it.

Green pea soup with chilled mint cream

Serves 6

1 medium Spanish onion, peeled and finely chopped
1 tbsp olive oil
3 tbsp unsalted butter
400g fresh peas, podded weight
1 small head of English lettuce, finely chopped
100g washed baby spinach
2 tsp caster sugar
850ml chicken stock
Maldon sea salt and freshly ground black pepper
150ml whole milk
¼ tsp ground nutmeg

Not the meaty pulse stew that we associate with winter nosh, but a really delicate summer soup that would not look out of place at the smartest lunch or dinner parties. Go for the freshest produce you possibly can and make double the quantity you need – it will keep splendidly for a few days, and will be a welcome 'ready meal' for that busy day when you're too knackered to cook when you get home.

Method

Use a heavy-based saucepan to sauté the onion until soft over a medium flame with the oil and butter. Add the peas, lettuce, spinach, sugar and stock and season lightly. Cover and simmer for 15 minutes on a low to medium flame until the peas are tender. Pour into a blender and process until fine, then add the milk and nutmeg and season again. Back in a saucepan, reheat (taking care not to boil the soup) and serve in bowls with a swirl of the mint cream.

Chilled mint cream

300ml single cream, chilled
a pinch of Maldon sea salt
4 tbsp finely chopped fresh mint

Method

Simply blitz all the ingredients in a processor on fast blend for 3 minutes until the mint is finely processed. Chill until required and pour onto the centre of the pea soup.

Salad Daze

In the Nosh philosophy, salads have always been regarded – quite rightly – as a side dish. Perhaps unfairly, you might say, as some salads can be quite substantial; and here, at least, we would concur. As a result we have included some guides to making salads part of your main course with examples like Salad Niçoise. (It takes a grilled slab of protein to elevate a peasant regional dish from France to a hallowed place in the Nosh salad repertoire.)

We have exploited their versatility to the full. They can be used as in between course items, starters in their own right, or simply accompaniments with crunchy textures to refresh the palate between mouthfuls.

A couple of warm salads have been included. Who said we can't have these in the summer months? Indeed, as we write, grey clouds have overcast the sky – a typical coolish summer's day. In fact, we can't remember a Wimbledon tournament when it didn't threaten to shower!

Salads can include meat or fish as part of the fun – here we have combined some beef with leaves and relied on unusual combinations of flavourings, like coconut, to complete the dish. The average supermarket has a wealth of different oils and vinegars on offer now, and you should spend time investigating these and experimenting with flavourings, for example wasabi instead of horseradish or mustard, and with some of the exotic leaves from the orient – there's more to salad than the traditional English limp lettuce, cucumber, slice of watery tomato, salad cream and a scattering of mustard and cress!

A recent trip to Spain has taught us the value of a proper mayonnaise – a field in which the Spanish are real experts. Take the time and trouble to make yours at home and use the fresh herbs that are available all year round now.

At the end of the day, a successful salad is about top-quality ingredients. Use the best oils and vinegars for dressings and the produce must be picked at the peak of ripeness and be of first-class quality – so don't expect too much from second-grade vegetables bought from the street markets. Make it fresh as you need it and don't let it stand wilting in the heat.

Recipes

Gado-gado

Peanut sauce

120ml peanut or sunflower
oil

4 cloves garlic, crushed and
chopped

360g peanuts, processed
fine

4 tbsp mild curry powder

1 tbsp sweet mango
chutney

1 small chilli, deseeded and
finely chopped

120ml lime juice

4 tbsp soy sauce

575ml coconut cream

500ml water

Vegetables

500g white cabbage, cut
into narrow strips

4 carrots, cut into thick
julienne strips

24 small new potatoes,
peeled and boiled

400g beansprouts

400g French beans,
trimmed

400g sugar snap peas,
trimmed

200g broccoli florets,
cut small

This is Indonesia's version of warm salad, and you can vary the vegetables used according to the season. However, the ones usually used are beansprouts, potato, green beans, carrots, and white cabbage. Here we have added sugar snap peas, and – to give a crispy texture – apple.

Sauce method

Place the oil in a heavy-based saucepan over a medium heat, add the garlic and the peanuts and cook for 2 minutes, stirring frequently. Add the curry powder and the chutney and chilli and cook on for another 2 or 3 minutes. Next, add the lime juice, soy, coconut cream, and water and simmer for 30 minutes, stirring frequently to prevent sticking and burning. Decant the sauce into a bowl and keep warm while you prepare the salad vegetables.

Salad method

The idea of the salad is to blanch all the vegetables in boiling water (the potato having been pre-cooked to make it tender), for about 2–3 minutes so that they do not lose their crunchiness. The easiest way to cook the vegetables if you're in a hurry is to cut them to a size that will make sure they are equally firm at the end of the blanching. Ensure that the carrots are not woody and the French beans do not have any stringy bits that would spoil the dish. Drain them thoroughly and serve them on warm plates, with the peanut sauce on top.

Niçoise-style salad with red pepper and orange dressing

60g black olives

60g cherry tomatoes

90g green French beans, boiled then refreshed in ice water

120g small new potatoes, boiled

4 hard-boiled eggs, shelled and halved

120g mixed salad leaves

1 teacup CLASSIC VINAIGRETTE (page 170)

4 x 100g firm-fleshed tuna steaks, grilled

2 tbsp chopped chives

Niçoise simply means 'in the regional style of Nice'. Ideally situated on the French Riviera for great weather, views and seafoods, the area enjoys the best of all worlds when it comes to eating out. What could be better than a fish soup followed by a grilled fish salad, featuring the catch of the day? We have specified tuna here, because it is easily available in England, but you could just as easily use mullet, bream, or any other firm-fleshed fish in season. The salads along the coastal region of Provence have many variations and it is perfectly acceptable to try out your own combinations. The main thing to remember is that all ingredients should be of prime quality – and use real mature black olives, not the supermarket ersatz tinned version that are pitted green ones and then dyed black with food colouring. Keep a close eye on timing, as well: don't over-boil the potatoes or beans.

Method
Arrange the vegetables and the eggs in the mixed salad leaves, dress with vinaigrette, and place the grilled fish on top of the salad. Garnish with the chopped chives and serve with the red pepper and orange dressing.

150ml FRUIT DRESSING (page 171)

1 red pepper, roasted, skinned and decored

Maldon sea salt and freshly ground black pepper

Red pepper and orange dressing

To the Fruit dressing add the finely chopped pulp of the red pepper. Blend in a mixer for 30 seconds to make a smooth dressing and check the seasoning.

Serves 3

10 ripe best-quality
   plum tomatoes (or
   5 beefsteak tomatoes)
4 tbsp best-quality
   extra-virgin olive oil
Maldon sea salt and freshly
   ground black pepper
a pinch of Italian dried
   herbs
3 'balls' fresh bufala
   mozzarella*
2 spring onions, thinly
   sliced
1 small bunch basil,
   shredded
a few drops of aged
   balsamic vinegar

** Normal cow's milk
mozzarella will do OK,
but the flavour of buffalo
cheese is worth the extra
expense and the texture
is much better too!*

Roast beef tomato, bufala mozzarella, spring onion, basil and balsamic

A variation here on the classic tomato 'n' mozzarella salad. English tomatoes are too bland usually to get good results, so roasting them with some olive oil and herbs helps to up the flavour quotient. Don't be scared to experiment yourselves – and do spend the extra money and effort in getting the bufala version of the cheese. It really makes all the difference from the rubbery industrial pizza-versions.

Method

Ensure that the tomatoes are bought perfectly ripe – they must be firm and red. They are to be roasted after having been dressed with olive oil and seasoned.

Wash the tomatoes and dry them. Next, cut horizontally along the long centre line of the tomato (bisecting it from stem point north to south). If the stem end has a very white hard pith core, remove it with a sharp paring knife and discard it. Arrange the tomato halves cut side up on a wire cake rack (*not* on a flat baking tray, as they will tend to burn on the bottom surface). Brush each cut surface with olive oil and season with sea salt, a twist of freshly ground black pepper, and a sprinkle of the herbs.

Bake in a preheated oven (190°C/375°F/gas mark 5) until they have roasted and shrivelled somewhat – this should take anywhere from about 25 to 40 minutes depending on size, but check from time to time that they are not scorching.

Assembly

Alternate slices of roasted tomatoes and cheese on a round display plate, sprinkle with onions and seasoning, then drizzle with olive oil and basil. A few drops of balsamic vinegar will finish the dish.

Serves 6

Greek salad

2 Cos lettuce, washed,
    drained, and cut into
    narrow strips
2 red onions, peeled and
    cut into thin rings
1 cucumber, peeled, cut
    into slices/chunks
10 tomatoes (ripe and good
    flavoured, e.g. beefsteak,
    cherry, or plum)
225g feta cheese (Greek
    preferred), marinated
    is OK
120g Kalamata olives
juice of 2 lemons
Greek extra-virgin olive oil
2 tsp oregano
3 tbsp chopped flat-leaf
    parsley

Rib-eye of lamb

6 x 120g pieces of
    well-trimmed rib-eye
    fillet of lamb
2 tbsp olive oil
1 tbsp oregano
freshly ground black
    pepper
juice and chopped squeezed
    peel of 1 lemon
Maldon sea salt

Warm Greek salad of grilled rib-eye of lamb

Here's an idea that we invented to allow us to enjoy the two best things about Greek cuisine we like – the lamb and the Greek salads. We have combined the two items into one warm salad. Greek lamb is, frankly, well flavoured but as tough as old boots; English lamb is much more tender than the scrawny efforts gambolling up the Greek mountainsides. There's something rather romantic about swigging retsina watching a few boats bob up and down in a white stone harbour under a blue sky. Shut your eyes and imagine you're there . . .

Method

Spread the Cos lettuce leaves on a large serving dish and assemble the onions, cucumber, and tomatoes on it. Arrange the feta and olives, squeeze with lemon juice, drizzle with olive oil and sprinkle with the oregano and parsley.

To cook the lamb, rub the meat with the olive oil and oregano, and season with pepper. Squeeze the lemon juice and the chopped peel over it and marinate for 30–60 minutes. Salt the meat and grill it for 5 minutes on a high heat to seal it (or until the outside is well cooked and there is a pink medium-rare nature to the centre). Greeks tend to cook everything to well-done, but then their meat is poorer quality than ours. When grilled, rest the meat for 5 minutes to allow the fibres to relax and then with a very sharp carving knife slice long strips on the bias to get diagonal lengths. Drape the lamb neatly around the salad and serve.

Warm Greek salad of grilled rib-eye of lamb

Fillet of beef salad with coconut mint dressing and croutons

1 kg fillet of Scotch beef,
   larder trimmed (free
   of all sinew and skin,
   and chain off)
8 tbsp olive oil
Maldon sea salt
1 tbsp coarsely crushed
   black pepper
2 slices stale white bread
Maldon sea salt and freshly
   ground black pepper

Salad
mixed salad greens
juice of 2 limes
2 tsp Thai fish sauce
175 ml coconut milk
6 tbsp peanut oil
2 tbsp finely chopped mint
1 small red medium-hot
   chilli, deseeded and
   finely chopped

This is a kind of East-meets-West 'fusion' dish that has inspired new ideas in British cooking. Not content with Chinese or Indian influences, Britons have looked futher afield to Malaysia and Australasia to steal ideas, and some are decidedly hit and miss. Some, however, hit the mark. This hit the bull's-eye.

Beef and crouton method

Preheat the oven to 200°C/400°F/gas mark 6.

Rub the fillet with a light smear of oil, some salt, and all the crushed black pepper. Let it rest for 30 minutes while the oven heats and you prepare the croutons. Cut the slices of bread into 1cm cubes and fry in 6 tbsp of the olive oil in a frying pan until golden brown, then drain on kitchen paper and reserve for the final assembly.

Wipe out the crouton pan with kitchen paper and heat until hot on a high flame. Sear the fillet on all sides to seal the flesh, then place it in a roasting tray, season, and cook for 15–20 minutes depending on its thickness. (You should aim for a medium-rare result.) Rest the beef on a cold plate for 10–15 minutes to relax the meat fibres before carving it.

Salad method

Using fresh ingredients ensures a good result. Red oak-leaf lettuce or batavia is decent although you can get new exotic salad leaves like shungiko (a dwarf chrysanthemum), mizuna, or the very esoteric types like, texel, tatsai, gold orach, serrated santo, celtuce and jaba. Green salad should be picked clean, washed and drained. It is vital that it is dry (a shake within a clean tea towel will ensure this).

The dressing is easy. Simply place all the liquids in a blender and process for a few seconds until all ingredients are thoroughly combined. There is a fair degree of saltiness in the fish sauce so no extra salt should be needed in the dressing.

Assembly

Toss the salad greens with thinly sliced strips of fillet in the dressing and then toss through with the croutons. Serve immediately before the dressing splits and the leaves wilt.

Warm carrot, hazelnut, and orange salad

Serves 8

800g sweet carrots
2 tbsp extra-virgin olive oil
1 tsp strong clear honey
juice of ½ a lemon
1 tsp grainy mustard
125ml CLASSIC
    VINAIGRETTE
    (page 170)
2 oranges, peeled and
    segmented, juices
    reserved
120g hazelnuts, shelled,
    toasted, and chopped
    coarsely
Maldon sea salt and freshly
    ground black pepper

Carrot salad is generally something boring that is added to green salads by clumsy English mass-caterers when they run out of inspiration, like throwing cress over Iceberg, or pickled beetroot slices on mixed salads (where a vinegary flavour overpowers all else). Here, we give a guide to a simple way to get the best out of a noble vegetable. The original salad we tasted in this style had fresh chopped tarragon in it. Neither of us are overly fond of it, and it's usually used in too much quantity, so here it's been dropped in favour of a nutty honey dressing.

Method

Peel and cut the carrots into thin batons, twice the thickness of julienne matchsticks and as long as the carrot's length will allow. Mix together the olive oil, honey, lemon juice, and mustard and add to the vinaigrette with the orange juice.

Blanch the carrots in boiling salted water for 1 minute and drain in a colander. When drained, but while still hot, place in a mixing bowl and toss with the hazelnuts and orange segments and drench with the dressing. Season and serve while still warm. The warmth helps to drive the taste into the carrots, which absorb the flavours.

Roasted red peppers and basil

**Makes 4 salad portions
or 12 crostini portions**

4 large or 6 small red
    peppers
3 tbsp olive oil
150ml extra-virgin olive oil
2 cloves garlic, peeled and
    chopped
1 small bunch basil,
    shredded
Maldon sea salt and freshly
    ground black pepper
1 large loaf CIABATTA
    (page 65 – optional)

Red peppers are in danger of having a taste bypass operation if the consumers don't wake up. The signs of pimiento fatigue are already showing and it is imperative that we demand the best. The smooth outlines of those mass-produced Dutch peppers are well known to us all and spell death to the taste buds. Go instead for the wrinkled and misshapen efforts from Spain and Italy which, although ugly to the supermarket buyer's eye, are beauty to the taste buds. If we don't speak up, we may relegate the pepper to the space reserved in the casualty ward for other patients of the vegetable world, courgettes, tomatoes, and most French apples.

Method

Coat each red pepper lightly with basic olive oil and place on the barbecue uncovered on the hottest part for about 8 minutes turning them over a few times to ensure even roasting. A kettle-type gas barbecue is perfect for quickly heating to roasting temperature – and you can see the progress of the peppers so much more easily. If you are roasting the peppers in a domestic oven set the heat to maximum.

The skin of the peppers should be slightly charred and bubbling, which makes it easy to separate the skin from the flesh. Don't overdo them, or the flesh will roast too hot and you'll end up with a very mushy result. If you're using an oven, preheat it to the maximum temperature and blister them for about 10–15 minutes. When done, remove to a cool high-sided tray and place the peppers in even layers with clingfilm tightly over the top of the tray. When cool, you'll find they'll peel easily.

Core and skin them then mix them with a little extra-virgin oil, the garlic and some basil, and season. Turn the peppers over . . . by hand . . . gently, so as not to break them up, and let them rest for the flavours to amalgamate.

Serve in a shallow serving dish with some more basil on top, or lightly brush the top side of seasoned ciabatta with extra-virgin olive oil and toast on the barbecue grill for a few minutes until golden brown. Then place some peppers on top, decorate with some fresh shredded basil leaves, and hand them around as guests arrive.

Potato salad with apple, egg, and pancetta

Serves 6

about 1 kg small new
  potatoes (Jersey Royals
  are the best)
3 good quality crisp eating
  apples (Braeburns are
  good)
6 spring onions, sliced
  thinly on the diagonal
Maldon sea salt and freshly
  ground black pepper
250g thin sliced smoked
  pancetta (barbecue-
  grilled, crisp and diced
  into lardons)
about 450ml MAYONNAISE
  (page 21)
a small bunch of chives,
  chopped

Here's a sample of salad that has its roots in Germanic cooking. It has a strong flavour which scored high on the Noshometer. If the mayo seems a little too stiff to cover the potato, thin it a little with some lemon juice.

Method

Wash the potatoes free of excess papery flaps of skin and then boil them in their skins in salted water until they are soft but retain a waxy middle with some bite. Plunge immediately into ice water briefly, and when cool to the touch, cut in half.

Peel and core the apples and slice into small dice. Add the spring onions, and season, then combine with the pancetta. Add the potatoes and the apples, and combine gently by hand but thoroughly to prevent the potatoes breaking up. Add the mayonnaise at once to prevent discoloration, and sprinkle over the chives.

Salad Daze

Pineapple coleslaw with tequila mayo

Serves 8

½ tsp Maldon sea salt

3 tsbp caster sugar

2 tbsp Dijon mustard

1 teacup sour cream

2 tbsp fresh lemon juice

1 teacup TEQUILA MAYO

1 medium white cabbage, finely sliced

4 pickled jalapeño chillies, stemmed and minced

3 spring onions, peeled and finely chopped

½ a medium pineapple, cored, sliced, and finely chopped

Mass-produced coleslaws always disappoint. The mayo used to bind them is too thin and vinegary, the cabbage is cut too short, and the result is a mess. Here's the antidote to all that. A million miles away from the 'industrial' blend of cabbage, carrot, and apple, it packs a real Tex-Mex punch and the tequila mayo and jalapeños give it a bite. Try it with the ribs and chilli-dogs in the barbecue section.

Method

Combine the salt, sugar, mustard, sour cream, lemon juice and mayonnaise and mix thoroughly. Next, add the cabbage and chillies to the liquids and combine thoroughly.

Refrigerate for at least 1 hour and add the spring onions and pineapple just before serving.

Tequila mayo

½ tsp freshly ground black pepper

1 tsp dry (yellow powdered) mustard

1½ tsp Maldon sea salt

1 tbsp tequila

3 tsp lime juice

2 tsp Cointreau

juice and zest of 2 medium oranges

4 egg yolks

300ml corn oil

Method

Combine all the ingredients except the oil in a processor and blend until smooth. With the machine still running on full power, pour in the oil in a reasonably quick, smooth stream. Check seasonings and adjust as necessary. This mayonnaise will keep in a fridge in a covered plastic container for 3 days.

Seaside Specials

Fish is a brilliant choice for summer cooking as it is quick to cook, flavoursome, and stops you spending hours in the kitchen when you'd rather be on the beach. Whether you wrap a salmon fillet in foil, or grill steaks, squid, or prawns over hot coals, fish and shellfish are the perfect choice. For ease of eating, choose fish with no small bones (you're more likely to find recipes with monkfish in than herring listed here).

Oily fish like salmon, tuna and halibut need little extra treatment; however, blander white fish may need marinating with flavoured oils, citrus juices, or an oriental paste like tamarind. Don't underestimate the value, in taste terms, of such home-grown produce as crabs – they have loads of flavour and help to make a soup or salad memorable.

In search of flavours we have searched the globe for inspiration and the dishes in this section are culled from a variety of cuisines: Italy, Japan, Jamaica, Spain, Australia and Scandinavia. Read the recipes, imbibe the essence of what we are attempting to achieve, and be prepared to change the menu according to what's on offer in the marketplace. Keep your choice spontaneous and stay flexible – that's the key to success. One proviso, however, is that you should avoid frozen fish of any kind. Freezing changes the texture and sometimes renders the dish completely unappealing, as in the case of squids. With the revolution in airfreight times in recent years we can now benefit from fresh rather than frozen lobsters from Canada, prawns from Goa, swordfish from Madagascar, and grouper from the Caribbean.

With an increase in the number of farmed fish there is much more choice all the year round, but sometimes, sadly, at the expense of flavour. However, the animal farmed will often benefit from intensive rearing, for example mussels or oysters. A close eye is kept on potential pollutants and water quality, eliminating a modern anxiety that plagues us all, regardless of the region we inhabit. Fishmarkets often have the best deal and you should be a keen supporter of your local fishmonger – who, if wise, will advise and help you to make informed choices about what's the 'best buy'. But don't overlook the wealth of different species that inhabit our coastal waters and try some that may be new to you but are extremely good: John Dory, crayfish, snapper, hake, and others. Don't just go for the tried and tested plaice, whiting, cod and haddock, great as these are.

With stress on stocks and reduced quotas in the fishing world, the prices are tending to go through the roof every year and it's a difficult time for choosing fish – but choose well and with some help from these pages you'll have excellent results.

Recipes

Seared basil-marinated tuna steak with linguine nero and onion focaccia 114

Nosh summer chowder 116

Sushi selection with Miso ramen noodles

Rice

1 tsp Maldon sea salt

500g round-grained Japanese sushi ('sticky') rice

175ml mirin (rice wine vinegar)

Fish

60g each of the following very fresh filleted raw fish: salmon, tuna loin, 'fatty' tuna (from the skirt of the fillet), abalone, prawn, razor shell, halibut, octopus, salmon keta, oyster (cut very thin)

To serve

1 tsp wasabi paste* (horseradish mustard)

pickled ginger root

Sushi, raw fish on cooked ricecakes, has grown in popularity recently. Japanese food was for many years almost unapproachable for Brits due to the prohibitive pricetag – being the reserve of expense-account business lunchers – but now is even on offer at up-market sandwich bars as a lunch option. The only proviso when making it yourself is to buy absolutely the freshest fish available and to make it just before serving. The other thing worth mentioning is that if you stuff yourself with meaty fare at a luncheon, you'll find yourself in snooze territory very soon afterwards, whereas with sushi, any excessive consumption is rapidly digested and you'll find yourself quickly energized for the afternoon's fun and games. Strange but true.

Rice method

Bring a large pot of water to the boil and salt it. Add the rice, bring back to the boil, reduce the flame, and continue to cook on a slow simmer until soft. Drain, allow to evaporate dry for a few minutes, then decant into a wide, shallow bowl. Add the mirin and stir evenly into the rice with a wooden spoon. Allow to cool when the mirin is incorporated well.

Fish method

Ensure all fish is of prime quality and has been stored in transit in well-chilled conditions. Slice all firm fish very thinly and store under clingfilm until ready for assembly.

* Wasabi paste is sometimes bought as a dry powder, rather like English mustard, and you have to reconstitute it with water into a stiff paste. If this is the case, allow 10 minutes' resting time for the wasabi flavours to develop.

Assembly

Gather a cold dessertspoonful-sized lump of cooked rice and shape it in the palm of your hand into a small, neat, rectangular log. Place a small dab of wasabi paste onto the top as glue and layer a slice of the fresh fish of your choice. Arrange the selection on a large platter and serve with slices of pickled ginger root*(this will refresh the palate between sushis!).

Pickled ginger is a taste explosion in your mouth and is available in Japanese supermarkets in jars and vac-pac bags. It resembles pale smoked salmon slices as it traditionally has a slight pinky-red colour in the pickling juices which transfers to the slices of ginger. Tip: When the jar is finished, re-use the pickling fluids by replacing the ginger and steeping it in a fridge for 2 weeks before use. (The ginger root will have to be peeled and thinly sliced lengthways with a potato peeler first.)

about 100g ramen noodles

about 300ml miso soup
    stock* (strong flavour),
    depending on bowl size

1 tsp dark miso fermented
    beancurd paste

Topping

2 cooked king prawns
    (cut in half along the
    centre and deveined)

1 scallop, steamed and
    sliced thin

1 tbsp raw beansprouts

1 x 3cm piece julienne-
    grated raw daikon

1 x 5mm piece ginger root,
    finely grated

4 seasonal green leaves
    (spinach, pak-choi,
    or pea shoots)

30g fine diced firm
    beancurd

To garnish

a few pieces of wakame
    or Nori seaweed

2 spring onions, finely
    chopped

Miso ramen noodles

Miso is a fermented bean paste, produced in a fashion not unlike soy sauce, that has a very savoury flavour. The Japanese slurp miso soup from side bowls as an accompaniment to sushi-type meals and its warming properties help all that fish go down easily. Don't be tempted when making this at home to increase the amount of miso to heighten the flavour – it's quite salty and you could end up with a raging dry mouth and a thirst to match.

Method

Blanch the noodles in boiling salted water for a few minutes until soft but *al dente*. Heat the soup stock to near boiling, add the miso paste, and dissolve it completely.

Drain the noodles, arrange them in a bowl, spread over them the fish and vegetable toppings and beancurd and arrange them neatly, then pour over the soup stock and garnish with the seaweed and spring onion.

* To a traditional light chicken stock mix add: mouli (white oriental radish), coriander leaves, watercress and a small amount of ginger root, grated.

Serves 6

3 tbsp chopped dill

2 tsp Maldon sea salt

1 tbsp caster sugar

6 x 200g fillets of fresh
    halibut

1 tbsp ouzo (or anis
    liqueur)

24 asparagus spears

300ml HOLLANDAISE SAUCE

freshly ground black
    pepper

Smoked gravlax of halibut with fresh asparagus spears and Hollandaise sauce

Halibut are famous for being one of the largest fish caught in the sea. Recently, one was caught off the English shores, weighing over 450 lb, which took hours to cut up and prepare by a whole team of kitchen staff (the record is over 600 lb). They taste great and being rather an oily fish, like salmon, lend themselves readily to taking on flavours like herbs or smoke. Here, we advise a variation on an old theme, gravlax – fish cured with a mixture of sugar and salt in the Scandinavian tradition. Forsaking brandy for ouzo we have added a novel twist to the process.

Method

In a small basin, mix together the dill, salt, and sugar.

Trim all the skin and bones from the fillets and place them on a large platter. Paint with a thin layer of ouzo (or anis) and then sprinkle each side with the dill mixture. Cover with clingfilm and leave for at least 3 days for the juices to be extracted and the fish cured. It is OK to pile up the fish on top of one another so long as you turn the fillets every day. When you're ready to serve the dish, slice the fillets very thinly on the bias.

Cook the asparagus spears until *al dente* in well-salted boiling water, drain and refresh and cool quickly in cold running water and then drain well again.

Hollandaise sauce

4 tbsp white wine vinegar
12 black peppercorns
2 bay leaves
a pinch of Maldon sea salt
3 egg yolks
a pinch of cayenne pepper
90–140g unsalted butter,
    softened

Method

Pour the vinegar into a small saucepan, add the peppercorns, bay leaves, and salt, bring to the boil, and reduce by half the volume. Strain into a teacup and allow to cool to blood heat.

Place the egg yolks in a bowl over a hot water bain-marie and add the cayenne pepper and the strained liquid. Whisking continuously, add the butter in walnut-sized lumps, until the sauce thickens. (Do not allow the sauce to boil or contact the hot water underneath or it will curdle.) Keep warm until required for serving.

Assembly

To serve, arrange a row of spears on each plate. Spoon generous dollops of Hollandaise onto it and and arrange the cured fillets on top of the spears. A few grinds of black pepper completes the dish.

Salpicón

1 green pepper

1 long green chilli

450g large red ripe
tomatoes, seeded and
chopped

½ long ridge-type
cucumber, peeled,
seeded, and chopped

½ medium Spanish onion,
peeled and chopped

1 garlic clove, peeled,
chopped, and pulped

450g large cooked prawns

¼ tsp finely grated fresh
ginger

1 tbsp sherry vinegar

1 tbsp extra-virgin olive oil

150ml thick premium
tomato juice

150ml V8 vegetable juice

juice of ½ a lemon

about 1 tbsp fresh white
breadcrumbs (from
stale bread)

large pinch Maldon sea salt

freshly ground black
pepper

½ tsp hot chilli sauce
(to taste)

To serve

1 dressed cooked crab (at
least 120g white meat)

12–16 jumbo prawns

After our recent visit to Spain we managed to perfect a gazpacho recipe that had proper weight to it. Some cooks favour balsamic vinegar but we used the appropriate sherry vinegar to complete the Spanish theme. It was a good idea to add seafoods, and it was a complete surprise to find that in reality a real Spanish version of seafood gazpacho already existed called *Salpicón*. Checking the traditional Spanish version against ours, it was a relief to find we weren't far off target. The main difference was that in Andalucia, where the soup is a mainstay of the starter lists in restaurants, the tomatoes, onions, and all soft vegetables were top-quality. Sadly, in Britain, we don't enjoy those luxuries but you can make up for the shortcomings of our climate by using V8 Juice, which has the added zip of concentrated carrot, spinach, and celery juices.

Method

Roast the pepper and chilli in a preheated oven set to maximum for about 10–15 minutes. The skins should be slightly charred and bubbling, which makes it easy to separate them from the flesh. Don't overdo them, or the flesh will roast too hot and you'll end up with a very mushy result. When done, remove to a cool high-sided tray and place the peppers in even layers with clingfilm tightly over the top of the tray. When cool, you'll find they'll peel easily. Deseed them, core them, and chop into fine dice.

Place all the vegetables, prawns, and ginger in a bowl with the sherry vinegar and olive oil and rest for at least a couple of hours in the fridge. When ready to serve, blend everything together in a processor with the tomato and V8 juices, to ensure all the chunks are evenly broken down. Add the lemon juice, breadcrumbs, and seasonings, whizz around for another few seconds, and then taste. Try not to process the soup as fine as a purée, but leave the texture slightly coarse, or, alternatively, process half or two-thirds of the mix very smooth and add the coarser part last to give some texture. Add the hot sauce, gradually, so as not to overdo the heat.

Keep the soup chilled until needed. Serve in chilled bowls and

scatter some shredded crab meat with a couple of jumbo prawns for garnish. Some people add a cube or two of ice, but don't bother. It dilutes the soup and is only really there for effect. If the soup is well made and well chilled, it won't be in the bowl long enough to get warm!

Lobster with mango, mint and basil

Serves 4

exotic mixed leaves
(red chard, orach,
rocket, mizuna, etc.)
2 mangoes, halved and
sliced
3 tbsp best virgin olive oil
½ tbsp balsamic vinegar
1 tsp white truffle oil
Maldon sea salt and freshly
ground black pepper
1 tbsp unsalted butter
tail and claw meat of
2 x 500g lobsters,
trimmed into small
medallions
1 tbsp chopped mint
1 tbsp chopped basil

A favourite shelllfish gets the modern warm salad treatment with an exotic twist. Truffle oil, somewhat fallen out of favour from its overuse in the early nineties, has been brought back – in this case it's perfectly teamed with 'the top prawn'.

Method
Wash the salad leaves, and trim most of them to bite-size pieces, leaving a few whole. Arrange them on plates in a pile with a whole leaf in the centre. Place the mangoes neatly around the circle of salad leaves. Mix the dressing by whisking together the olive oil, balsamic vinegar and truffle oil and seasoning.

Heat the butter in a frying pan over a hot flame and sear the lobster quickly. Drain on kitchen paper and place the medallions on the mango and sprinkle with the chopped mint and basil. Stir the dressing and pour over the lobster salad in a generous manner. Finish with black pepper and serve immediately.

Smoked salmon pancakes with cider, and keta and Gruyère

Pancakes
230g plain flour
60g unsalted butter, melted
6 small eggs + 2 extra yolks
a pinch of Maldon sea salt
zest of ½ a lemon, finely
    grated
250ml Breton or dry Devon
    cider
250ml whole milk

Filling
1 tbsp cognac
600ml double cream
    (Channel Island is best),
    whisked
600g Scottish smoked
    salmon, sliced very
    thinly
400g Gruyère, grated

To serve
65g salmon keta
fresh chopped dill

An easy one this, with a twist in using cider for the batter. The strong flavours of salmon roe and Gruyère make for a substantial dish.

Pancake method

Place all the ingredients in a processor and blend well for 30 seconds. Leave to rest for 1 hour.

When the batter mix has rested, lightly grease a crêpe pan with butter and lightly cook each pancake on both sides on a medium heat. The mix should make about 35 pancakes. When the pancakes are cool, stack them with small pieces of greaseproof paper in between. Don't be tempted to stack the pancakes up while still warm – they will stick together and you won't be able to prise them apart without tearing and spoiling them!

Assembly

The pancakes are assembled in a pile with fillings in between so it resembles a cake.

On a lightly buttered baking tray place one pancake. Mix the cognac and cream together and spread a teaspoon of this all over the first pancake with a palette knife. Then spread a piece of smoked salmon on this and then a sprinkling of Gruyère. Now place a new pancake on top and repeat the process until you have a stack of about 8 pancakes in a pile. On the penultimate pancake, place a generous amount of cheese. Then bake in a preheated oven (200°C/ 400°F/gas mark 6) for about 10–12 minutes.

To serve, warm the remaining brandy/cream mixture and spoon over the pile(s). Place the keta on top with a scattering of chopped dill.

Serves 1

80g raw tuna, diced small

4 tbsp chopped rocket

1 tbsp chopped fresh basil

1 tsp garlic pulp

1 tsp small ('Lilliput')
  capers

juice of ½ a lemon

1 tsp virgin olive oil

a dash of chilli oil

4 or 5 premier-grade black
  olives

Maldon sea salt

freshly ground black
  pepper

200g angel hair pasta
  (capellini)

To serve

2 tbsp coarse grated
  Parmesan

Angel hair pasta with raw tuna, capers, and olives

Sydney always leaves pleasant memories of fine dinners and our last visit was no exception. We are indebted to Gerry and Denise D'Angelo for the following easy recipe, which was perfect for a substantial brunch to fight off any lingering hangover from the previous night. Gerry was last seen at The Sports Bard in Bondi – he will probably have his own place by now. Bondi is a fast-evolving centre for quick and easy dining out at very reasonable prices. Australian cuisine enjoys the best ingredients and the best of influences: the fabulous seafoods of Australian waters, Italian skills, and Asian spicing. This dish shows the simplicity and full flavours of a typical Sydney early morning lunch, lingering over the papers with an OJ and a cold beer, gathering energies for the dining marathon that lies ahead when darkness falls.

Method

This is intended to be a light summery dish that requires no cooking apart from the pasta – ingredients are simply folded into the cooked capellini and seasoned.

Mix together all the ingredients except the pasta, then cook the pasta for about 3–4 minutes in fast-boiling well-salted water. Fresh pasta will only take about 1–2 minutes, so don't overcook it – *al dente* is the way forward. Drain well and fold into the mixture of fish, herbs, olives and seasonings. Shaving a little Parmesan on top with a final grind of black pepper completes this delicious dish.

Angel hair pasta with raw tuna, capers, and olives

Jerked red snapper with sweet potato chips and red pepper mayonnaise

6 x 175g fillets of red
   snapper
1 tbsp each of plain flour
   and fine ground
   cornmeal flour, mixed
jerk seasoning (paste or
   powder)
Maldon sea salt
1 tbsp coconut oil
2 cloves garlic, peeled
juice of 1 lemon
4 spring onions, finely
   chopped
50g fennel, blanched and
   finely julienned
2 medium carrots, peeled
   and finely julienned
1 thin leek, cleaned and
   finely julienned
2 tbsp finely chopped
   spring onion
30g unsalted butter
100ml dry white wine

   To serve
a squeeze of lemon
a handful of chervil,
   chopped

1 kg sweet potato
peanut or sunflower oil for
   deep-frying
Maldon sea salt

In this dish, fish 'n' chips get the West Indian treatment. Instead of ketchup you have red pepper mayo and kumara replaces the trad King Edwards. Jerk seasoning is variable in quality and it is worth hunting out the real thing. Spurn the cheap ersatz copies of this fully loaded spice combination. If you can't get red snapper, use grey snapper or sea bass.

Fish method

Press each fillet lightly into the cornmeal flour mix, season with jerk seasoning and salt, and pan-fry in 1 tbsp of the coconut oil on a high heat, with the garlic. A couple of minutes should be enough on each side. Lift the fillets out (leave the garlic in the pan), squeeze lemon juice over them, and keep them warm on a roasting tray in a very low oven (130°C/275°F/gas mark 1).

Add the vegetables to the pan with the butter and sweat them over a medium flame, turning frequently to prevent browning. When soft, discard the garlic, add the wine and simmer for 1 minute. The juices will thicken slightly. Serve the fillets with a generous portion of vegetables, a squeeze of lemon and some sauce, and sprinkled with chopped chervil.

Sweet potato chips

When deep-frying these chips, take care not to have the oil too hot, or you wil scorch the chips and leave the centres uncooked. A deep-fryer (electric 'safe' type with lid) and basket set to 160°C/325°F is best.

Red pepper mayonnaise

2 red peppers
1 tbsp olive oil
150ml best quality olive oil
300ml good quality salad
    oil (e.g. sunflower)
3 small egg yolks*
Maldon sea salt
1–2 tsp good quality Dijon
    mustard
1 tbsp white wine vinegar
1 tsp lemon juice
freshly ground black
    pepper
a pinch of caster sugar

Method

Preheat the oven to maximum. Coat each red pepper lightly with olive oil and blister them in the oven for about 10–15 minutes. The skin of the peppers should be slightly charred and bubbling, which makes it easy to separate the skin from the flesh. Don't overdo them, or the flesh will roast too hot and you'll end up with a very mushy result. When done, remove to a cool high-sided tray and place the peppers in even layers with clingfilm tightly over the top of the tray. When cool, you'll find they'll peel easily. Deseed them then whizz them in a processor and allow to drain, so only the damp pulp is used (not too fine). Reserve.

To make the mayonnaise, mix the oils and whisk the egg yolks with some salt, the mustard and the vinegar. Drizzle in half the mixed oils, incorporating them thoroughly and beating all the time. Then add the lemon juice and continue to pour and whisk oil in. Finally adjust the seasoning, adding salt, pepper and sugar if necessary. If the mayonnaise looks too thin or has split and curdled, it is possible to rescue it by beating another yolk in a separate bowl and pouring the original mixture in gradually, beating well as before, but really taking plenty of time to whisk well together.

Then add the reserved peppers to the mayonnaise until the mixture is creamy red in colour, and adjust the seasoning.

Serve on the side as a dipping sauce for the sweet potato chips.

Important: if the processed red pepper is not drained, the sauce will become thin and watery!

To remove the worries and fears about any lurking salmonella in raw egg, simply mix the yolks with the vinegar at the start and leave for 5–10 minutes, stirring once or twice. Salmonella hate vinegar and it will reduce the risk of any contamination.

Serves 6

1kg whole red snapper,
 descaled and cleaned
polenta flour for dusting
2 red chillies, finely
 chopped
3 green chillies, finely
 chopped
1 x 2cm piece fresh ginger
 root
3 shallots, finely chopped
4 large cloves garlic, peeled
 and finely chopped
4 white peppercorns
4 black peppercorns
1 tsp coriander roots,
 cleaned and finely
 chopped
about 350ml peanut oil
6 spring onions, finely
 chopped
2 tbsp Thai fish sauce
3 tbsp tamarind water
1 tbsp jaggery (or palm
 sugar)
120ml thick coconut milk

To serve
juice of 1 lime

Tamarind snapper with spicy noodles

The tamarind has a naturally sour taste that lends itself to fish cookery easily. Here we cook a whole fish that is served on rice noodles in the Thai style. Hot chillies are *de rigueur* for this dish.

Method

Wash the snapper, pat it dry, and make three diagonal slashes in each side. Dust the fish with polenta flour and set aside. Meanwhile, with a pestle and mortar grind the red and green chillies, ginger, shallots, garlic, white and black peppercorns, and coriander roots until a smooth paste.

In a large wok, heat some peanut oil over a high flame until hot, and deep-fry each side of the fish for 6–8 minutes, turning only once. (Take care not to spill the hot oil and create a dangerous inflammable situation – safety first at all times in the kitchen.) Drain the cooked fish on kitchen paper.

Next, reduce the flame to medium and fry the spring onions until brown and crisp, and drain on kitchen paper. Reserve for garnishing. Stir-fry the spices paste in a small saucepan in 2 tbsp of oil, again on a medium-hot flame, then add the fish sauce, tamarind water, jaggery or palm sugar, and coconut milk, lower the heat, and simmer for 5 minutes.

Serve on a large platter. Make a bed of the spicy noodles, and display on it the fried fish. Squeeze the lime juice over it, spoon over the sauce, and then decorate with the crispy spring onions.

Serves 6

350g thin rice noodles

2 eggs

1 tbsp red chillies, finely
    chopped

3 shallots, finely chopped

4 tbsp peanut oil

4 tbsp tamarind water

1 tbsp light soy

1 tsp mild curry powder

1 tbsp Thai fish sauce

½ tbsp palm sugar

10 green prawns, cleaned
    and sliced small

2 tbsp dried shrimp

3 tbsp beancurd, diced and
    fried until crisp

2 tbsp chopped raw cashew
    nuts

2 tbsp mung beansprouts

1 spring onion, chopped

Spicy noodles

Method

At least 2 hours before the meal, prepare the noodles. This will give them time to dry out properly – wet, soggy noodles will stick together and clog the dish. Blanch the rice noodles in fast-boiling water to soften them. It is imperative that you don't overcook them: a minute is enough. Drain them, refresh them in a colander in ice-cold water, and drain them well again. This 'draining and turning over process' to dry is a crucial help to smooth stir-frying. Make an omelette with the eggs and allow it to cool, then cut it into fine julienne strips and reserve it.

Grind the chillies and shallots together with a pestle and mortar to make a paste, then heat the oil in a wok to very hot and stir-fry the paste. Add the tamarind water, soy, curry powder, fish sauce, and palm sugar. Bubble up and then add the chopped prawns and fry over a high heat until they change colour. Add the drained, dry noodles and toss evenly until they are well coated, and then add the dry garnishes (including the julienned omelette) and toss through roughly.

Serves 6

500g *bacalao*, soaked in
cold water for 48 hours
500g potatoes, cut to make
chips
olive oil for frying
1 tbsp chopped 'Lilliput'
capers

To serve
2 tbsp chopped flat-leaf
parsley

Bacalao with a tomato and red onion salad with a truffle oil dressing

Mick Nosh was intrigued one summer's day by some fishy mashed potato served at The Chelsea Arts Club. Tony the head caterer was quizzed, and the secrets of *bacalao* (salt cod) were briefly explained. The way to get the best results, as with any salted item, is to ensure that the soaking process is not skimped on. You will need to wash the excess salt from the *bacalao* under running cold water, then let it soak in fresh cold water for 48 hours, changing and discarding the water every 6 hours. And don't forget to double check for bones – it saves on lawsuits!

Method

In a large pan of fresh water, bring the fish to the boil and then simmer for 10 minutes. Allow to cool in a basin of cold water until cold enough to handle, while you make tomato salad as below. Then strip the skin and fins from the cod, taking care to discard any bones. Flake the fish and reserve. Next, fry the potato chips in medium-hot olive oil until they're soft and cooked throughout but not crisp!

Mash the chips into the flaked cod, add the capers, then mix to make small fishcakes. Fry in hot shallow olive oil for a couple of minute to heat up, and then place on top of the tomato salad and serve with a sprinkling of parsley.

Tomato and red onion salad

6 large salad tomatoes

Maldon sea salt and freshly
    ground black pepper

4 spring onions, chopped
    finely

1 tbsp raspberry vinegar

2 tbsp virgin olive oil

1 tbsp truffle oil

You want only the tastiest tomatoes, whether they're beefsteak ones or salad toms – choose ripe firm fruits.

Blanch the tomatoes in boiling water, skin them, and chop them into eighths. Chill then season them. Sprinkle fine pieces of spring onion over them.

To make the dressing, dissolve Maldon sea salt in the raspberry vinegar and then add the olive oil and mix thoroughly together. Finally, add the truffle oil which will give a richness and a depth to the tomatoes.

Serves 4

1 tbsp unsalted butter

6 tbsp virgin olive oil

400g old potatoes, peeled
    and mandolined thin

4 tbsp sage, finely chopped

Maldon sea salt and freshly
    ground black pepper

175g coarsely grated
    Parmesan

400g hake fillet, free of
    bones

Hake baked with potatoes, sage and Parmesan

Often made Down Under with sea perch, this is a substantial dish with origins in Spain, Italy and the Western Mediterranean. It's simple and uncomplicated to cook. In fact, it needs a real idiot to muck it up. Hake is a particular favourite of the Spanish, but samples in Britain are often supplied frozen – so shop carefully.

Method

Preheat the oven to 190°C/375°F/gas mark 5.

Grease a lasagne-style baking dish with butter and sprinkle with some of the olive oil. Place a layer of potato about 1cm maximum depth over the bottom of the dish and then some sage and seasoning, and then cheese and fish. Sprinkle with more olive oil and then repeat the layering process until the dish is full. (About 4 layers maximum is probably best.) Finish the top layer with fish, oil, and sage. Cover the dish with foil and place in the oven for 25 minutes. Then take off the foil cover and continue for another 20 minutes or so until the potatoes and fish are cooked through and the top layer is slightly crisped.

Seaside Specials

Serves 4

Infused-oil

10 tbsp chopped fresh basil leaves and their stems

10 tbsp best-quality olive oil

6 tbsp virgin olive oil

3 small red chillies, deseeded and finely sliced

4 cloves garlic, thinly sliced

2 whole cloves

6 black peppercorns

4 bay leaves

zest of 1 lemon

2 tsp 'Lilliput' capers

1 tbsp chopped flat-leaf parsley

6 black olives, stoned and coarsely chopped

4 tuna loin steaks, trimmed of all skin and bone

400g black (squid-ink) linguine (linguine nero)

To serve

Maldon sea salt and freshly ground black pepper

Seared basil-marinated tuna steak with linguine nero and onion focaccia

Modern fashions have dictated that old complicated sauces should be avoided in favour of flavoured oils and simple dressings. This is a typical example of that type of dish. Black pasta seems strong on the eye at first, but (thankfully) is also strong on the taste buds. Searing is not an affectation: don't overcook the tuna, or the juices disappear and it's pointless.

Infused-oil method

Mix the basil leaves into the best-quality olive oil and and let the tuna steaks marinate in it for 1 hour. Warm the virgin olive oil with the chillies, garlic, cloves, peppercorns, bay leaves, lemon zest, and basil stems and let them flavour the oil for 30 minutes or so. Do not let the flame get high enough to cook them, simply allow the flavours to infuse. Strain the oil and add the capers, parsley, and olives. Keep the oil warm for the assembly.

Tuna method

Season the tuna steaks and grill on a very hot griddle or barbecue. Sear the steaks quickly to seal the juices in then cook for 2–3 minutes each side for rare to medium-rare.

Pasta method

Cook the black linguine in well-salted boiling water on a rolling boil until tender (with a slight bite *al dente*), then drain well.

Assembly

To serve, toss the black linguine in the infused olive oil with plenty of black pepper, make a bed of it, and arrange the tuna steaks on top.

This is supposed to be a rich dish so don't worry about the high density of olive oil . . . it's deliberate.

Onion focaccia

Method

Follow the instructions for olive focaccia on page 16, substituting 120g finely sliced Spanish onion rings for the olives.

Nosh summer chowder

Serves 6

750g mixed fish fillets
(snapper, eel, whiting,
bream, salmon, etc.)
500g shelled seafood
(mussels, prawns, squid,
crab, langoustines,
scallops, etc.)
1 small Spanish onion,
peeled
1 bulb fennel
2 leeks, cleaned (include
some pale green flags)
2 cloves garlic
4 tbsp olive oil
1 tbsp fennel seeds
1.1 litres fish stock
2 medium potatoes, peeled
and finely diced
2 tsp saffron strands
150ml fresh single cream
Maldon sea salt and freshly
ground black pepper

We both love fishy bouillabaisse-type stews, but frankly they are a bitch to deal with, as regards the bones. To enjoy this type of dish as fully-flavoured as we think it should be, we have specified a strong fish stock be added to fish fillets. When cooking is complete, the soup will have some thickening from the potato, fine flavours from the fish and vegetables and the orangey-yellow colour from the traditional saffron with a coarse texture that's free from bones – thus a chowder . . . as it should be and . . . Heaven!

Method

Ensure that all fish pieces and shellfish are clean and free of all bones, shell and grit.

Chop the onion, fennel, leeks and garlic and sauté in the oil in a deep-sided frying pan on a medium flame for 10 minutes until soft and well cooked. Place the fish pieces and shellfish in the pan, add the fennel seeds, stock, potato, and saffron and bring to the boil, then simmer slowly for 40 minutes until the potato has started to disintegrate and thicken the juices into a chowder. Then add the cream and stir roughly with a fork to loosen the texture of the soup. Chowder should be a chunky soup and not a broth so don't be tempted to liquidize it in a processor.

The chowder is designed to be served hot, but the best flavours evolve when the soup is allowed to cool for say, just 10 minutes before serving.

This is a substantial soup and with the addition of some bread may become a meal in itself!

On Yer Hols

Holidays are one of our main inspirations for bringing back new ideas to try at home in our kitchen. Idyllic moments, however, are harder to recreate than you think. Who hasn't lingered over a lunch of grilled fish and salad in a Greek harbour on a sunny day swigging retsina and enjoying the sunny ambience? Bringing the retsina home and having a barbecue in Britain is a bit of a shock – retsina simply doesn't travel. There is a silver lining, however, to every dark cloud. British meat is usually tenderer than the wild Continental stuff and there is a trade-off here for flavour vs texture.

Having said that, we are always looking to improve what we have had on our vacations abroad and Greece is a good starting point. Moussaka. Brilliant and a favourite, but sadly lacking in any finesse. If you follow our recipes listed in this section, you can experience what must have been at the core of the Ottoman idea it first started out as – we have Noshed it up with extra spices and yogurts in the white sauce – a far cry from the cold, cracked white slab of draught-excluder moussaka that can pass for a supper dish on holiday. Similarly, we love the concept of stuffed peppers, even though our plastic supermarket efforts are not up to Italian or Spanish standards. Usually, the peppers are stuffed with bland rice 'n' spice ingredients which don't pass close scrutiny. Here we've attempted to stuff the peppers with strong fish, shellfish, and robust flavours like lemon that will have more than a passing effect on your taste buds.

So in this section we have tried to recreate for you the best of what we have found on our hols, with a decent stab at the proper ingredients and seasonings and with a critical eye on the method of cooking to bring you the optimum results – to recreate properly 'in the comfort of your own home'.

Not all supermarkets have reasonable deli sections yet, and for some of the Italian produce you may have to look around for a decent shop for your salsicce or top-grade Parmesan. They will also have a supply of the more exotic produce you may need, such as quails, rabbits, or salted vine leaves. Whatever your requirements, always choose the freshest produce and don't be frightened to ask for advice – and *experiment*!

Recipes

Singapore noodles with Char siu roast pork

360g rice noodles (fine
    vermicelli rice noodles)
2 tbsp peanut oil
2 spring onions, sliced 1 cm
    long (on the diagonal)
1 red pepper, finely sliced
1 green pepper, finely sliced
1 small red chilli, sliced
    thinly 'across the grain'
6 king green (raw) prawns,
    heads off, deveined, and
    halved
3 tbsp small shrimp, cooked
    and peeled
½ tsp sugar
½ tsp Maldon sea salt
¼–½ tsp mild curry
    powder (no more!)
a handful of beansprouts
60g CHAR SIU ROAST PORK
2 eggs, beaten
1 tbsp light 'clear' soy
few drops chilli oil

Much copied, seldom executed well. It's a personal favourite of Mick Nosh that demands a light touch with the spices and the oil. The secret to a successful rice noodle stir-fry is to ensure that the blanched noodles are dried out very well before use, otherwise they stick to the sides of the wok.

Method

Blanch the noodles for 10 seconds, refresh them in ice water for 20 seconds, drain them dry, then chill them. It is important that the noodles are soaked yet not soggy. When dry they should be teased apart so they don't clump together. Frequent turning will ensure they dry out evenly.

It is imperative that the wok is heated up fully before the oil is poured in. When it is really hot add the oil and stir fry the vegetables, then add the prawns and shrimp and cook until the shellfish are nearly done. Add the noodles, sugar, seasoning and curry powder, then beansprouts, pork, and eggs. Moisten with the soy and chilli oil and serve at once on hot plates.

Char siu roast pork

350g 'larder trimmed' pork
    fillet
1 tbsp red bean curd
    'cheese'
1 tbsp dark soy
½ tbsp yellow bean paste
1½ tsp peanut oil
1 tsp sugar
1 tbsp Chinese wine

Your butcher should supply you with pork fillet ready trimmed and cleaned. If it's untrimmed, use a very sharp knife to remove all fat and sinews, including the chain that runs the length of the fillet. The fillet is usually bought whole, and weight varies from 240g to 360g, depending on the size of the pig. You can keep any unused pork in the fridge in an airtight container for 3 days.

Method

Rub the pork with all the other ingredients and marinate for 1 hour.

Roast brushed with oil on a roasting tray for 5–7 minutes in a preheated oven (190°C/375°F/gas mark 5). When cool, slice into 2mm strips.

Serves 3

1 egg white
30g cornflour
120g green (raw) prawns, peeled and deveined
180g fresh scallops, cut in half (across 'equator')
120g fresh squid (cleaned and sliced, tentacles included)
peanut oil for frying
1 x 120g can Chinese water chestnuts, drained, sliced into 1cm discs
6 white stems Chinese leaves, chopped large
2 spring onions, chopped, on the diagonal
6 large fresh shiitake mushrooms
2.5cm piece fresh root ginger, sliced
2 cloves garlic, crushed
½ tsp salt
a pinch of caster sugar
100ml chicken stock
1 tbsp Chinese wine or dry sherry
a few drops of sesame oil

Seafood stir-fry, Chinese leaves, ginger, and spring onions

Why bother to get a take-away, when you can cook this classic of Chinese dishes without having to put up with the offhand manners and surly service of Chinese restaurateurs? This dish tastes as good when we make it as some of the best meals we've had in Hong Kong (although we haven't been back since they gave it back to the Chinese – what were they thinking of?).

Method

Mix the egg white and cornflour together, and reserve a quarter of the mix. Thoroughly mix the seafood into the remaining three-quarters, then stir-fry it in the oil for about 2 minutes and drain on kitchen paper. Reheat the wok and cook the vegetables, herbs and seasoning, adding dashes of stock until the dish has a generously moist but not soupy consistency. Add the wine or sherry and the reserved egg/cornflour mix to thicken it up, combine everything together, add the sesame oil and serve immediately.

Serves 4

1 large bunch Chinese
    broccoli
1 tsp peanut oil
2 cloves garlic, peeled and
    finely sliced
400ml light chicken stock
good quality 'imported'
    oyster sauce

Chinese broccoli with garlic oyster sauce

Broccoli, we think, is just a side dish. In any other form of cooking it should remain just that. This sprouting broccoli is rather special though and demands proper treatment – and in our view is worthy of a place on the main plate. But follow the instructions below, otherwise you'll end up with just another side dish. You'll need a wok lid for this method.

Method
Trim the bottom edges of the broccoli and remove any white flowers from the sprouting tops.

Heat the oil in a wok over a high flame, and when hot, throw in the whole stems of broccoli. Keep the stems moving rapidly to prevent burning and after 30 seconds throw in the garlic. Keep the whole thing moving constantly, as even garlic slices burn and turn bitter if they're not kept on the move. After another 30 seconds pour in enough stock to keep a source of steam emitting from the base of the wok that will be enough for the whole batch to be steamed in – half the 400ml at least should be used. Add more if your wok needs it. Cover with a lid and steam/braise rapidly for about 2–3 minutes or until the thickest stem of broccoli is cooked through (testing with a knife is OK but you may need to test it with your teeth to really ensure correct cooking throughout).

To serve, shake a couple of generous squirts of oyster sauce over the veg – it will melt into the dish nicely.

Salsicce with polenta, tomato and basil sauce

Serves 5

2kg salsicce

750g medium-grade
    polenta (the slow-
    cooking type)

1.1 litres TOMATO AND
    BASIL SAUCE (page 67)

120g unsalted butter

To serve
shavings of Parmesan or
    Fontina

Salsicce piccante are spicy peppery pork sausages. In London, a good supplier is Camisa in Old Compton Street, London W1 (0171 437 7610). Their links are tied off with brown butcher's string, which is very distinctive (they have a natural casing). They have a coarse texture and need careful slow cooking, to ensure the interior is done well. They are delicious served with the tomato and basil sauce. There are various 'instant-cook' types of polenta which are sometimes fine grade and can be cooked within a few minutes; these are OK but don't have the texture and flavour of the premier-grade type which usually takes about 20 minutes to cook through properly, with a lot of stirring so that the cornmeal doesn't catch and burn on the bottom of the pan.

Method

Remove the string ties to prevent them catching alight and grill the sausages under a medium flame. Slow grilling helps prevent bursting of the sausage casings – so take it easy. Keep them warm when they're done.

The polenta is cooked in plenty of boiling salted water (follow the directions on the packet) to achieve a mashed-potato-type consistency. When the polenta is cooked, mix the butter into it, spoon it onto a warm plate, place a couple of salsicce on top, ladle a generous portion of tomato sauce on them, and grate a few shavings of Parmesan over.

Any polenta that is left over will soon set solid, so spoon it onto greaseproof paper while still warm to a depth of 2cm or so and let it set into a slab. You can then cut it into sections and reheat it by painting it lightly with olive oil and grilling it (either under a grill or on a hot ridged griddle set over a medium high flame on the hob). Also, you can place slices of cheese on top and bake it in a preheated oven (230°C/450°F/gas mark 8) for about 5 minutes, until the cheese has melted.

Salsicce with polenta, tomato and basil sauce

Mediterranean stuffed peppers

Serves 4

4 large firm red peppers

3 tbsp olive oil

2 large fresh white closed-
cap mushrooms, sliced

360g fresh monkfish, diced
small

250g green (raw) king
prawns, heads off and
peeled

1 clove garlic, finely
chopped

3 spring onions, coarsely
chopped (with their
green flags)

2 tbsp chopped flat-leaf
parsley

a pinch of dried rosemary

juice and zest of ½ a lemon

1 large ripe tomato,
skinned and medium
diced

Maldon sea salt and freshly
ground black pepper

To serve

1 onion, finely sliced

1 tbsp olive oil

chopped flat-leaf parsley

Generally speaking and notwithstanding the decline in the quality of red peppers available from supermarkets, we both agreed we liked roasted stuffed peppers as a concept. But unfortunately, most efforts (usually eaten on holiday in the Med) were dull and stuffings revolved around rice, maybe a few herbs or so but always ended up bland – the worst sort of vegetarian food. So we took the challenge in hand and whacked a few major fishy items inside. Also we weren't frightened to properly roast the whole peppers. They may collapse a bit more on the plate but at least would have that specific sweetness that they should have – most efforts only 'show them the cooker'. Looking great without taste isn't worth a damn.

Method

Wash and dry the peppers. Slice the top off each one (reserve it to make a lid) and scoop out the seeds. The idea is to stuff the peppers with the lightly cooked mixture, place the lids of the peppers back on and bake in a hot oven for 25–30 minutes.

For the stuffing, heat the olive oil in a frying pan over a hot flame and quickly seal and cook the mushroom, monkfish, and prawns for about 3 minutes, adding the garlic after about 1 minute. Remember, the contents will be roasted further so don't overcook the fish or it will dry out. Transfer the contents of the pan to a bowl and combine with the spring onion, herbs, lemon juice and zest, and the tomato. Season well and stuff with a small teaspoon into each pepper, pressing down with the back of the spoon to ensure even packing (during cooking the peppers will sag and lose their shape), and replace the lids. Place in a small baking dish so they are tightly packed and upright, and roast in a preheated oven (200°C/400°F/gas mark 6) for 30 minutes, depending on size. Meanwhile fry the onion in the olive oil until dark brown and crisped up. To serve, take off the lids and sprinkle with the crispy onion and parsley.

Moussaka

960g best minced lamb
(lean, not fatty)

3 Spanish onions, finely
chopped

4 cloves garlic, peeled and
crushed

good olive oil

3 cans tinned plum
tomatoes, drained

1 small tube tomato purée

4 tbsp oregano

2 tsp ground cinnamon

Maldon sea salt and freshly
ground black pepper

4 large aubergines

4 large floury potatoes

1.1 litres béchamel sauce*
(made very stiff)

3 eggs, whisked

300ml whole fat Greek
yogurt

120g fresh grated Parmesan

Love it. But why do the Greeks, supposedly the arbiters of all things traditional in this area, muck it up with bland sauces, and then serve it cold? Tepid is OK, but *cold* . . .? We have taken the original essence of the Ottoman tradition in which this dish originated and elevated it back to the correct level (and beyond) using cinnamon and yogurt in the sauce.

Method

Sauté the lamb with the onion and garlic in 6 tbsp of the oil until cooked lightly. Add the tomatoes and tomato purée, the oregano and half the cinnamon, season and reserve.

Meanwhile, slice the aubergines thickly, sprinkle salt copiously over them and leave them in a colander over a bowl for about 1 hour to let the bitter juices escape, then wash, drain and dry them. Pan-fry them over a medium flame in olive oil until light brown on both sides. Parboil the potatoes and skin them, then slice them while still hot into 3mm slices. Mix the béchamel with the remaining cinnamon, the eggs, and the yogurt.

To assemble the moussaka, place the slices of potato on the base of the dish (this will absorb any excess juices), then some mince, then some aubergines, repeating and adding the tomatoes, finishing with an aubergine layer then a thick layer of béchamel sauce, and Parmesan for topping. Bake in a preheated oven at 190°C/375°F/gas mark 5 for 40 minutes.

* To make a full-flavoured sauce, simmer the milk for the white sauce first with a large onion, bay, cloves, peppercorns and a little mustard and then infuse off the heat for 1 hour. This, when strained, will provide a strong base for the béchamel.

White onion pizza

Serves 6–8

Pizza dough
1 kg plain strong flour
  (for breadmaking)
3 tsp Maldon sea salt
2 tsp caster sugar
2 sachets easy-rise yeast
  granules
2 tbsp olive oil
300 ml lukewarm water

Topping
2 white onions, peeled and
  thinly sliced
3 small packets of bufala
  mozarella (about 90g
  total), sliced
4 tbsp virgin olive oil
1 tbsp oregano
Maldon sea salt and freshly
  ground black pepper
a big handful of chopped
  flat-leaf parsley

Pizzas have evolved into a staple of the British way of life, but not many people try to make their own. It's a shame really, as most manufactured versions are rather industrial in their appeal. Pizzas also have the advantage of being appealing to children who have not yet fully 'evolved' their adult taste buds – it's a bore having to make two types of food for the family so try this white onion version. It's gourmet and yet 'comfort food' – at the same time!

Method

Mix the dry dough ingredients in a large bowl and make a well in the centre. Add the olive oil and 200ml of the water and stir well with a wooden spoon. Add the remainder of the water gradually until a smooth round ball of dough has gathered. (You may not need all of the water.) Leave in a warm place, covered with clingfilm, until the dough has doubled in size.

Preheat the oven to maximum. Roll out a ball of dough as big as a fist until it is about 5mm thick and 23cm across, then set it on a heavy flat baking tray. Spread a small handful of the onion slices and mozarella slices over the base and sprinkle them with the olive oil and oregano. Season and bake for 10–15 minutes, until the onions are cooked but not burnt and the pizza base is crispy. Scatter some parsley on the top, slice into wedges, and serve hot.

Goat's cheese and rocket pizza

Pizza dough
220g plain flour
60g rye flour
1 sachet easy-rise yeast
    granules
½ tsp Maldon sea salt
2 tbsp whole milk
1 tbsp olive oil
150ml lukewarm water

Topping
3 crottins (fresh goat's
    cheeses), each sliced
    into 4 discs
2 tbsp virgin olive oil
freshly ground black
    pepper
1 tsp oregano
a handful of baby rocket,
    washed and chopped

Pizzas have evolved from their simple tomato 'n' cheese toppings and the following recipe is a favourite. You can substitute Gorgonzola if you don't like the sourer taste of the goat's cheese; it is an acquired taste – but we prefer it like this.

Method

Mix the flours, yeast, and salt in a large bowl and make a well in the centre. Add the milk and olive oil and 100ml of the water and stir well with a wooden spoon. Add the remainder of the water gradually until a smooth round ball of dough has gathered. (You may not need all of the water). Knead the dough for 10 minutes to allow the texture to become even. The dough should be moist but soft.

Place in an oiled bowl and leave in a warm place, covered with clingfilm, until the dough has doubled in size. Before using punch it down and allow to rise for another 40 minutes.

Baking

Preheat the oven to maximum. Roll out a ball of dough as big as a fist until it is about 5mm thick and 23cm across, then set it on a heavy flat baking tray. Spread the goat's cheese slices on the base and sprinkle them with the olive oil, black pepper, and oregano. Bake for 10–15 minutes until the cheese is cooked but not burnt and the pizza base is crispy. Scatter the rocket on the top where it will wilt with the residual heat of the pizza, slice into wedges, and serve hot.

Serves 4

3 large red chillies

1 red onion, finely sliced

6 tbsp coriander leaves, chopped

4 tbsp olive oil

2 tbsp tequila

juice of 3 limes

1 tbsp liquid hickory smoke

6 x 240g chicken breasts, skinned and boned

2 large red peppers, seeded, cored, and julienned

1 Spanish onion, peeled and thinly sliced

Maldon sea salt

6 floury tortillas

300ml CLASSIC SALSA

300ml GUACAMOLE

To serve

FOUR-BEAN 'FRIJOLES REFRITOS'

Chicken fajitas with four-bean 'frijoles refritos'

This is an excellent way to serve marinated barbecued chicken in warm tortillas with salsa and guacamole with peppers and onion. The use of liquid smoke gives a real 'outdoor barbecue' feel to this dish.

Method

Blend the chillies, red onion, coriander, half the olive oil, tequila, lime juice, and liquid smoke in a blender, then marinate the chicken breasts for about 2 hours at room temperature.

Meanwhile prepare the peppers and onion by cooking them in the remaining oil in a heavy pan until soft (about 10 minutes over a high heat). Season when ready. Replace on the grill to keep warm until the fajitas are ready for assembly.

To cook the fajitas, chargrill the chicken for about 12 minutes or until done, and then cut each breast into thin strips across the grain. (Add any meat juices from the cutting board to the onion and pepper mixture in the pan.) Warm the tortillas.

Assemble by placing on each warmed tortilla some chicken, then peppers and onion, then salsa, and finally a dollop of guacamole. Roll and fold the flaps of the tortilla to make a neat long parcel and enjoy while still hot. Serve with the 'frijoles refritos'.

Classic salsa

2 long green chillies

2 large ripe tomatoes, skinned, cored, seeded and chopped

4 large spring onions, finely chopped (including flags)

Salsa has overtaken ketchup in the USA in sales, it's so popular. The manufactured product available in the UK still leaves something to be desired, so we recommend walking briskly past that part of the aisle and getting your own ingredients. Try to get the best available tomatoes – after all, they're the keystone of the dish.

a handful of coriander leaf,
chopped
3 tbsp fresh-squeezed lime
juice
1 tbsp olive oil
½ tsp Maldon sea salt

Method
Roast the chillies over the hottest part of the grill and turn them until they're evenly charred. Leave in a bowl covered with clingfilm until cool then peel away the skin, remembering not to touch your face or eyes with your hands – and then wash your hands thoroughly. Now coarsely chop the peppers.

Stir together all the ingredients in a large bowl and refrigerate for 1 hour. Adjust the seasoning.

Guacamole

4 large black-skinned ripe
avocados, pitted and
peeled
2 fresh jalapeño chilli
peppers, deseeded and
finely chopped
5 ripe plum tomatoes,
deseeded and diced
small
5 fresh spring onions, sliced
small
1 tsp Maldon sea salt
a few drops of Tabasco or
hot chilli sherry
small handful of chopped
fresh coriander leaves
(no stems)
2 tbsp sour cream
juice of 2 limes

Everyone has their favourite way of making guacamole. Generally speaking, most home-made efforts are OK but some of the supermarket versions leave a lot to be desired. Guacamole is something that should be made freshly and it should have a coarse texture – usually, the supermarket versions taste industrial, and have all the texture of sterilized baby food. Avocados that have 'gone over' are the usual choice for making this dish, but try to buy some specially, chosen for being firm but ripe. The other argument continues – small dark wrinkly variety or the large smooth green Israeli ones? It doesn't really matter so long as you have ripeness as avos are, in themselves, blandish – indeed in the later days of the British Empire, the Royal Navy used to feed their crews on them after visits to the Caribbean. They were called Midshipman's Butter and considered rather poor food. Here, though, we have elevated the humble fruit into a taste experience. Try it yourself.

Method
Combine all the ingredients. The secret is to use ripe avocados and crush them roughly with a fork. Processing the mix, like some 'industrial' versions, is a no-no. As the avocados eventually discolour and the mix goes grey, make this one at the last possible moment. It will not keep without eventually going black in colour.

Serves 4

575 ml chicken stock
1 x 360g can of borlotti
    beans, drained
1 x 360g can of lima beans,
    drained
1 x 360g can of haricot
    beans, drained
1 x 360g can of kidney
    beans, drained
2 tbsp olive oil
2 cloves garlic
3 tbsp chopped coriander
    leaf
60g unsalted butter

Four-bean 'frijoles refritos'

The 'frijoles refritos' (recooked beans) dish is our own adaptation of the Mexican classic, using a modern selection of different beans to get more variation in taste and texture. You can, of course, attempt to cook the beans 'the long way round', i.e., soaking, rinsing and all that palaver. It's very noble if you want to, but frankly, we don't have the time. Just make sure you shop for the very best quality in pre-prepared goods.

Method

Heat the stock in a saucepan and stir in the beans. Meanwhile, heat the oil in a large saucepan over a medium flame, crush the garlic in, and stir for a couple of minutes without browning it, then add the beans and stock mixture from the other saucepan. Crush the beans with a potato masher and keep the mixture turning over, 'frying' them lightly, with a wooden spoon. When all the beans have been cooked through (the stock will be mostly absorbed) add the coriander and a knob of butter. Serve hot with the fajitas.

Paillard of veal with Brazil nut sauce

3 tbsp olive oil

60g unsalted butter

4 x 180g fillets of veal
('butterfly cut', beaten
flat into escalopes, and
lightly floured)*

Maldon sea salt and freshly
ground black pepper

Sauce

60ml dry white wine

100ml Marsala

300ml single cream

1 tbsp lemon juice

6 tbsp Brazil nuts, toasted
and grated

To serve

2 tbsp Brazil nut shavings

Open any sixties cookbook and you'll notice the wealth of veal recipes – casseroled, roast, or in fillets. Veal's image has suffered somewhat from farming methods that did not endear the product to the British public. Now, it's time for a renaissance, particularly as you can get veal on the bone (up to 30 months of age). Try this one – it's very easy and veal has a great texture that's difficult to spoil. The nut sauce is an unusual combination to try. To soften nuts for easier shaving, boil them for a few minutes then use a potato peeler to make shavings.

Method

In a very large frying pan or flat griddle, heat the olive oil and butter over a high flame; when the butter is sizzling, sauté the veal fillets for 3–4 minutes until brown. You may not be able to fit them all in the pan, so remove them and cook the rest, keeping the meat warm until required for serving.

To make the sauce, add if necessary a little more butter to the pan and stir in the meat residues and then add the white wine to deglaze it. Stir around briskly and add the Marsala. Bring to the boil then reduce to a slow simmer, adding the cream and lemon juice until the sauce thickens. Then add the nuts and keep warm. Spoon the sauce over the veal to serve, season, and sprinkle with some nut shavings to finish.

* Veal fillets are quite small in cross-section – and even if beaten quite thin and flat will only make a circle of meat about 12cm in diameter. By 'butterfly cutting' the fillet you can stretch the potential size of the piece to an impressive and respectable 20cm or 23cm, depending on your dexterity with a knife. Cut almost through each slice and then upturn the fillet and repeat the cut on the other side – slightly further down – to make a 'zig-zag' of fillet, which when laid flat and pressed, beaten or rolled will make a large-sized fillet.

Just Desserts

As a pair who prefer savoury to sweet things we have had to really stretch ourselves to bring you some new ideas for the sweet bit after the cheese! Apart from treating themselves to complicated desserts when dining out, most people seem to hanker after simple desserts that, psychologically, remind them of nostalgic childhood favourites. You don't need much prompting to list them here: chocolate cakes, apple pies, sticky puddings . . . In this section we have endeavoured to present a few novel ideas that don't always fit this rigid label: for instance, gin and tonic ice-cream was not on my list when growing up – although it should have been! Where we have used a traditional dessert idea such summer pudding as a starting point, we have Noshed it up with special ingredients or liqueurs to add layers of extra flavour. Heavy stodgy concepts have been spurned in favour of granitas, mousses, and caramel custards whose lighter textures lend themselves to the seasonal approach. Check out the exotic appeal of black rice bavarois – rice pudding with a twist!

Many people think that making desserts is beyond their capabilitites. Sometimes it does seem a bit daunting, like making flaky pastry – well, just buy ready-made, there's nothing wrong with cutting some corners. But ensure if you are following that ready-made route that you really do insist on the best quality. For instance, fresh filo pastry is much better to handle and gives better results than frozen.

A simple Genoa cake you've bought can be transformed with the addition of juices, fruit liqueurs, and jams into a great base for a dessert. Much better, though, is to end a great meal with a selection of fresh fruits and cheeses that complement it, and one of the recipes we have given here is perfect with cheeses of all types. It's an apricot cheese, a preserved paste-in-a-slab that takes the place of a more savoury pickle or chutney.

It's well known that fresh air sharpens the appetite, and if that's the case then your guests will have no trouble in finding room for some of the offerings we've given here.

Recipes

Pink champagne ice-cream

Serves 10

16 medium egg yolks

200g VANILLA SUGAR
(page 139)

750ml rosé champagne
(Laurent Perrier is
good)

1 litre double cream
(Channel Island is best)

200g liquid glucose

A preference for pink champagne has historically been seen by most people as either slightly decadent behaviour, rendolent with a caddish whiff of the thirties or to the wine buff slightly wussy, verging on Nancy-Boy Potter territory, taking place alongside fussy jewellery, petits fours, doilies, wicker wine baskets and the like. But here the more delicate appeal suits this light summery ice.

Method

In a glass bowl beat the egg yolks until smooth and combined. Strain out in a fine sieve to remove any dark nuclei or threads and return to the bowl. Add the vanilla sugar and continue to beat together until the mixture goes pale and creamy. Now add 500ml champagne to half the cream and bring it to the boil. Add the glucose, remove from the heat (turning down the flame to very low) and quickly whisk in the sugar and egg mixture until dissolved thoroughly. Keep whisking for about 1 minute then transfer the saucepan back to the very low flame and simmer, stirring all the time with a wooden spoon for about 5–6 minutes or until the mixture has thickened and will coat the back of the spoon. Next, remove from the stove and pour in the remaining champagne and cream, which will rapidly cool down the process and arrest the cooking. Cool rapidly in a large plastic container and refrigerate in a deep freeze (stirring once after 1 hour) until firm.

Allow to warm up for 10 minutes if very solid for easy scooping. Nice served with biscuits like tuiles or macaroons.

Caramelized mangoes and papaya with gin and tonic ice-cream

Serves 6

60g caster sugar
2 tbsp water
60g unsalted butter
3 firm mangoes, peeled,
    cut into large slices
3 firm papayas, peeled,
    cut into large slices

To serve
chopped mint

Daydreaming about the tropics inspired this combination of two favourite things, tropical fruits and gin and tonics. Usually, in the shops, exotic fruits are either too hard to eat immediately or too soft and overripe to peel easily and turn to mush in your hand. Here we can take advantage of the over-firm fruits by cooking them.

Method

In a small frying pan melt the sugar in the water, then turn the flame up high to caramelize the sugar syrup into the dark caramel that has that distinctive smell as it's about to 'turn'. As that aroma appears add the butter to make a rich sauce, and place the fruits in the syrup and cook quickly for only 1–2 minutes, taking care not to reduce them to a mush. When the fruits have been covered in the sticky toffee-like sauce they can be sprinkled with chopped mint and served with a couple of scoops of the gin and tonic ice-cream.

Gin and tonic ice-cream

Serves 10

16 medium egg yolks
200g VANILLA SUGAR
1 litre double cream
    (Channel Island is best)
400ml Schweppes tonic
    water
200g liquid glucose
75ml gin

Tanqueray is one of the best for drinks and cocktails but the higher level of alcohol makes for a difficult freezing time. For this recipe you will need a strong-flavoured but standard-alcohol gin such as Bombay Sapphire.

Method

In a glass bowl beat the egg yolks until smooth and combined. Strain in a fine sieve to remove any dark nuclei or threads and return to the bowl. Add the vanilla sugar and continue to beat together until the mixture becomes pale and creamy. Now bring 500ml of the cream nearly to the boil, then add the tonic water and glucose and remove from the heat immediately. Turn down the flame to very low. Quickly whisk in the sugar/egg mixture until dissolved thoroughly. Keep whisking for about 1 minute then transfer the saucepan back to the very low flame and simmer, stirring all the time with a wooden spoon for about 5–6 minutes or until the mixture has thickened and will coat the back of a spoon. Next, remove from the stove and pour in the remaining cream, which will rapidly cool down the process and arrest the cooking. Now stir in the gin and cool rapidly in a large plastic container. Refrigerate in a deep-freeze (stirring once after 1 hour) until firm.

Allow to warm up for 10 minutes if very solid for easy scooping.

Vanilla sugar

Although one can split and remove the potent seed paste inside each vanilla pod, a simple flavouring is achieved by placing a couple of vanilla pods in a preserving jar with about 500g of caster sugar. The essence of the vanilla will seep into the crystals and it is a simple matter to turn the jar and shake it up every day for a week or two. After a couple of weeks the sugar reaches maximum potency and can be used here for other fine dishes like sprinkling on toppings and bread and butter puddings and basic custards.

Chocolate and mascarpone roulade

Serves 8

6 small egg yolks

130g caster sugar

200g dark Belgian or Swiss chocolate

2 measures extra-strong 'ristretto' coffee

7 egg whites

a pinch of Maldon sea salt

6 tbsp smooth apricot jam

250g mascarpone

1 tsp vanilla essence

Topping

icing sugar

160g finest grade Swiss/ Belgian milk chocolate

For the tin

oil, flour, caster sugar

Roulade is notoriously moist and has a tendency to 'crack' and break when rolling it up. Don't panic if this happens, just persevere and disguise the cracks with icing sugar – a certain rustic appearance is fine to complete the log illusion. Mascarpone gives a suitably rich and nineties feel to a classic idea. 'Ristretto' is Italian for restrained; the same amount of coffee is used as in an espresso, but only 50–65 per cent of the water. This is good for cooking as it imparts the strong taste without the quantity of liquid that would dilute the dish and spoil the taste.

Method

Preheat the oven to 200°C/400°F/gas mark 6.

Beat the egg yolks and the sugar until the mixture goes pale and creamy. Melt the chocolate with the coffee in a saucepan and stir into the egg and sugar mixture. Now whisk the egg whites with the salt until stiff, but don't over beat. Stir a third of the whites into the chocolate mixture thoroughly, then fold in the next third to lighten the mixture and the last third very loosely. Cut some greaseproof paper slightly wider than your Swiss roll dish and oil, flour, and sugar it. (This will help to detach the finished baked roulade.) Spread the mixture evenly over the Swiss roll dish with a palette knife and bake for about 12 minutes or until the top is slightly browned and firm to the touch. Leave to cool, covered with a damp tea towel (this will prevent the roulade from drying out). Now, using the palette knife, spread a thin layer of apricot jam over the surface (this will stop the mascarpone melting into it). Whip the mascarpone up with the vanilla essence and spread over the jammy surface, then, using the protruding edge of paper, roll up the slab like a Swiss roll, removing the greaseproof paper as you go.

Dust the final log with icing sugar, and to decorate melt the chocolate and pour onto a clean, cold kitchen surface (stainless steel

Summer Nosh

is best) that has been lightly oiled. The chocolate will cool and when cold can be scraped up with the flat blade of a knife to make scrolls and 'bark' pieces that can be used to top off the roulade.

Melon ice-cream

Serves 8

30g VANILLA SUGAR
    (page 139)
120ml hot water
250ml grated ripe
    cantaloupe or galia
    melon
1 tsp Midori liqueur
5 small egg yolks (at room
    temperature)
60g caster sugar
300ml double cream
    (Channel Island is best)
    whipped medium stiff
1 tsp very finely chopped
    fresh mint

To serve
½ melon, scooped with a
    small ice-cream scoop
    into balls

Here's a light, fruity dessert that makes full use of the melon liqueur Midori. Midori as a drink, even with mixers, is a bit lightweight and on the sweet side – 'a girl's drink,' a barman once said. Combined into this, however, it's quite appropriate for a cooling dessert.

Method

Make a sugar syrup by combining the vanilla sugar and the hot water and bubbling it on a high flame until it forms a thick syrup. If you have the luxury of a sugar thermometer it should read 110°C. Reserve the syrup aside to cool. Meanwhile, sprinkle the grated melon with the Midori liqueur and chill.

When the syrup is cool, whisk it into the egg yolks until fluffy and then fold in the sugar, cream and mint. Place in a deep-sided plastic container in the freezer for about 2–3 hours and then remove from the freezer and whisk in the grated melon mixture and freeze again until firm. This will probably take 2–3 hours. Then, using a small ice-cream scoop, ball out the ice-cream and mix with the melon balls.

Serves 6

White chocolate orange mousse

300g 'luxury' white
    Continental chocolate

4 tbsp caster sugar

3 egg yolks, at room
    temperature

7 egg whites, at room
    temperature

a large dash of Cointreau

zest of 2 oranges (no bitter
    white pith) dissolved in
    30ml boiling water,
    macerated and strained
    to make orange essence

White chocolate, although tasty to nibble, spells death to the taste buds in cooking, because it has none of the dark cocoa mass, so we have Noshed it up with Cointreau and orange essence. The liqueur lends some of its strength to the sauce which complements the dessert nicely.

Method

Break the chocolate into little squares and place in a bowl over some hot water to melt. Do not overheat or you'll coagulate the chocolate. Whisk half the sugar with the yolks until smooth and creamy. Then, with a clean dry whisk, whisk the whites until stiff and foamy and then add the remaining sugar and continue to beat together. The secret here is to add the sugar towards the end, otherwise, if added too early, the whites will not stiffen into peaks. On the addition of the sugar the peaks will take on a glossy look and you should then add the Cointreau and the orange essence. Then divide the egg whites into 3 separate dishes.

Add the melted butter to the melted chocolate and remove the pan from the heat. Now the timing is crucial.

Once cool materials are added to the chocolate mix the mousse will start to solidify, so rapid whisking is required.

First, fold the yolk and sugar mix into the first dish of egg whites and mix thoroughly but gently. Then add the chocolate and butter mix quickly and mix thoroughly together to blend the chocolate without any chips appearing.

Next, to give volume, gently fold in the second dish of egg whites with a large spoon and stir around. Finally add the third dish of egg white, folding very gently to distribute the whites evenly and keep the mousse as light as possible. Work lightly with upwards movements to get as much air as possible into the bowl and don't overwork each stage. Stop as soon as the whites are fully incorporated. Pour the mousse mixture neatly and quickly into a serving bowl, or individual ramekins or dessert glasses, and refrigerate for a couple of hours before serving. This is such a 'full-on' recipe for

mousse you can pour them into eggcups and you will be surprised how filling the dessert is! Remove the mousse 15 minutes or so before serving – it's best well chilled, but not so cold as to kill the flavour.

Apricot cheese

Serves 6

1.5 kg fresh ripe apricots
250 ml water
450 g sugar

This dish originated in Spain, where it is made with quinces and called *dulce de membrillo*. It is not a dessert in the strict sense of the word but a paste that when set can accompany good cheeses. Here we have used the theme to create an apricot paste that fulfils the same idea. To make a substantial dessert, simply place a couple of slices of Dolcelatte or Cashel Blue on some fresh halved and peeled pears, and grill until the cheese melts. Serve with freshly shelled walnuts with some strong Greek mountain honey spooned over them. A slab of the apricot paste on the side is perfect.

Method

Wash, dry, and halve the apricots, removing the stones. Chop roughly and put in a preserving pan with the water. Simmer until tender and then push through a coarse sieve or mouli to create a rough purée. Now add the sugar and gently stir and simmer the mixture for about 40 minutes until the mixture is quite thick. (The paste should detach itself from the sides of the pan like a choux pastry.)

Pour the paste into a crockery mould about 4 cm deep, cover, and leave to rest for 24 hours at room temperature. When it's firm, turn out into greaseproof paper and then refrigerate in foil. It should keep for 2 months.

Chilled caramel and apple soup

Serves 6

80g caster sugar
260ml cold water
260ml dry cider
½ tsp fresh grated root
    ginger
zest of ½ an orange
juice of 1 lemon
1 vanilla pod, split and
    seeds removed
1 kg Braeburn apples,
    peeled, cored, and
    grated, to give at least
    500g net weight fruit

To serve
single cream

Chilled soups loom large in the memory of childhood summer foods, and watercress, asparagus, leek and potato, gazpacho and even cold redcurrant soup remain fond favourites. However, it's time to experiment a little and this one was developed with a view to a savoury/sweet combination. It really needs to be chilled thoroughly, though.

Method
Stir the sugar and water together in a saucepan over a medium flame until the sugar dissolves. Then boil over a high heat, without stirring, until the sugar caramelizes to a dark golden brown colour. Then into the syrup pour the cider, ginger, orange zest, lemon juice, vanilla paste (the seeds from the vanilla pod) and apple and bring to the boil. Then simmer for 15 minutes or more to allow the apples to disintegrate. (Use a power whisk if necessary to help homogenize the soup.) Sieve into a large bowl and chill for 2–3 hours after cooling. Served into individual bowls you can add a swirl of fresh single cream.

Nectarines in syrup with Grand Marnier sabayon

Serves 8

8 large firm but ripe
    nectarines, washed and
    stoned, skin on
½ bottle Muscat de Beames
    de Venise
4 tbsp vanilla sugar
2 vanilla pods
small blade of cinnamon

To serve
clotted cream

The taste of peaches is sublime but many can't stand the furry texture on biting through the skin. Nectarines are different, however, in that they don't have that furry, felt-like covering. So whether eating raw or cooking them they're the perfect choice. To accompany this dish we'll specify a sabayon sauce, or as the Italians call it, *zabaglione* (pronounced 'zab-ba-ley-*oh*-nay'), sometimes written 'zabaione' (it's the Italian version of the French sabayon sauce, comprising egg yolks whisked into a hot mixture of fortified

wine and sugar). Here we use Grand Marnier, the sweet orangey liqueur from France. Zabaglione dates from the seventeenth century, where in Turin, one of our distant ancestors, Guiseppe Nosh, the chef to Carlo Emmanuel of Savoy, accidentally invented this dish by pouring some fortified wine into a custard mix. It was a great success and was dedicated to San Giovanni Baylon, from whom its name derives.

Method

Place the nectarines in a saucepan with the wine, sugar, vanilla pods and cinnamon and bring to the boil slowly. Then simmer for 5 minutes or so until the nectarines are tender. Don't overcook the fruit or you'll get jam!

Remove the cinnamon and discard it, take out the nectarines and set aside. To make the sauce, reduce the wine on a high heat until it has a syrupy texture and becomes viscous, then return the fruit and let it cool until you're able to refrigerate it.

Serve chilled with clotted cream or for extra luxury some of the Grand Marnier sabayon sauce.

Grand Marnier sabayon

6 egg yolks
4 tsp caster sugar
6 tbsp Muscat de Beames
    de Venise
10 tbsp Grand Marnier
zest of 1 lemon

Method

The dish is made by whisking all the ingredients together over heat: the mixture should thicken up gradually and eventually resemble a foamy golden custard. The best result comes from using a stainless-steel bowl some distance from a high flame, but you can do it safely in the top half of a double boiler, taking care the upper bowl does not touch the water. The custard should thicken and leave 'strands' where the balloon whisk is dragged through it.

Nectarines in syrup with Grand Marnier sabayon

Serves 6

1 litre whole milk
zest of 2 oranges
 (no white pith)
400g caster sugar
200ml cold water
20 blood orange segments
 (no white pith)
8 small eggs
4 tbsp Grand Marnier
unsalted butter

Orange crème caramel with blood oranges

Despite its sixties connotations crème caramel is still very much in vogue on the Continent – not so much as a retro dish, but as a time-honoured favourite that has never disappeared from classic restaurant menus. In Spain, where the bittersweet caramel juices and custardy pudding are still much enjoyed, it is often referred to as crème Catalan. We've Noshed it up using orange zest with another sixties sweet-trolley classic – caramelized oranges. Grand Marnier adds a touch of gravitas.

Method

Bring the milk and orange zest to the boil in a large saucepan, remove from the heat and leave to infuse for about 10 minutes. Meanwhile, make the caramel.

Stir 275g of sugar and the water together in a saucepan over a medium flame until the sugar dissolves. Then boil over a high heat, without stirring, until the sugar caramelizes to a dark golden brown colour. Then pour the syrup equally into six metal moulds to a depth of 1cm, reserving the rest in the pan, warm. Place the blood orange segments into this warm caramel syrup and set them aside to chill on an oiled baking tray in the fridge.

When the milk has infused, strain it and discard the orange zest. Beat the eggs and remaining sugar until pale and creamy, then add the reserved milk and whisk thoroughly to combine. Stir in the Grand Marnier and strain the mixture through a fine sieve (to remove egg threads).

Butter the moulds above the caramel and pour the mixture into them. Stand them in a bain-marie (with water halfway up the sides) and bake in a preheated oven (200°C/400°F/gas mark 6) for 45–50 minutes until set but not solid: they should be slightly wobbly, as they will continue to cook on in their own latent heat as they cool. Remove the moulds from the water to allow correct cooling. Serve cold (not chilled).

Before serving, run a sharp knife around each mould and turn it out onto a flat plate. Decorate with the toffeed-orange segments and any surplus caramel syrup.

Caramelized pineapple flamed with rum

Serves 8

175g caster sugar
2 tbsp unsalted butter
2 large pineapples, sliced
250ml medium or dark
   rum

To serve
2 large pineapples,
   hollowed out

Get on your grass skirts for this one and do the hula-hula. An excuse to get out that pineapple icebucket and cocktail umbrellas, and review your holiday snaps from Miami. Take care not to ignite hair or clothing when torching the dessert.

Method

In a clean heavy-based frying pan dissolve the sugar in a dash of water over a low heat, then turn up the flame to high to caramelize the sugar, adding the butter when the sugar begins to turn to caramel and then reducing the flame to medium (to control the transition of the caramel more easily). The sugar will start to turn browner with that distinctive toffeelike aroma. Remember, don't overcook the sugar otherwise it will turn blackish and bitter (in that case you have to throw it away and start again!).

When it nears the toffeelike caramel spot, place the slices of pineapple in the pan. Continue to cook the fruit on a high heat, browning them in the caramel for about 5 minutes or so each side until cooked but not mushy. Next pour the rum into the pan and tip the spirit to one side, igniting it and flaming off the alcohol.

Serve in hollowed-out pineapples with lids.

Brioche summer pudding with kirsch

Serves 4–6

Kirsch syrup
60g caster sugar
80ml water
2 tbsp kirsch liqueur

Pudding
butter and sugar for
    greasing the basin
8 large slices brioche, crusts
    off (to fit the pudding
    basin sides and top)
150g warmed sieved apricot
    jam
900g untrimmed weight
    summer berries
    (blackcurrants,
    redcurrants,
    raspberries,
    strawberries, pitted
    cherries, etc.), trimmed
    of all chaff, stems, and
    pits

Caramel sauce
125g caster sugar
2 tbsp water
250ml double cream
    (Channel Island is best)
1 tsp Madagascan vanilla
    extract

Here's the deluxe version of a summer classic. Caramel sauce adds a distinct note of excess with the kirsch and short of adding a meringue on the side we couldn't make it richer. (Actually, a meringue sounds fine . . . now where did I put that whisk . . . ?)

Method

To make the kirsch syrup, stir the sugar and water together and bring to the boil in a small saucepan. Turn down the heat and simmer for 1 minute, then add the kirsch and stir. Cover and leave to cool for 2 hours then refrigerate until chilled. Reserve.

Grease the pudding bowl liberally with butter, then sugar it, and line the sides and then the bottom with thin slices of brioche loaf, ensuring that no holes are left for the fruit juices to escape. Keep some for the lid. Paint the inside of the slices with the jam to seal the pudding.

Mix the fruit well with the kirsch syrup and pour the mixture into the basin, sealing it with a lid of brioche slices. Place clingfilm over the top and a plate on top of that to press down and shape the pudding, then refrigerate it overnight. (The kirsch syrup and fruit juices will permeate the brioche and the pudding will have that distinctive purple-red colour.)

To make the caramel sauce, heat the sugar with the water over a medium flame until the sugar is dissolved, then turn up the heat to high and create a caramel that is dark golden colour and has that distinctive toffeelike aroma. Take the pan off the heat and add the double cream to dissolve the mixture. Add the vanilla extract. Stir briskly to dissolve all the caramel and create a simple sauce.

To serve, place the basin in a bowl of boiling water for a few minutes to warm the butter lining – then it can be carefully inverted and slid out onto a serving plate.

When cut, the slices will ooze kirsch juices onto the plate, where generous spoonfuls of the caramel sauce will complete the dessert.

Serves 4

Black rice and coconut bavarois

Coconut
150ml milk
75ml coconut milk
90g fresh coconut flesh,
    finely grated
1 egg yolk
30g caster sugar
1 tsp gelatine (dissolved in
    a little hot water)

Jaggery syrup
60g jaggery or palm sugar
60ml water

Rice
60g black rice, soaked
    overnight
150 ml water
a pinch of Maldon sea salt
a slice of root ginger, peeled

To serve
150ml double cream
    (Channel Island is best),
    whipped

Black rice sounds ominous, but isn't really. Coloured rice abounds in the Far East.

Black rice is simply an exotic variation of round-grained rice from the Far East (not to be confused with the wild 'black' rice from the lakes of Minnesota) and can be bought from specialist oriental delis. It is usually reserved for desserts and the combination with coconut is great either as a dessert or a breakfast dish.

Decent oriental delis should have supplies of this and the jaggery (palm sugar). Try and hunt them out – the subtle differences make all the difference.

Method

Bring the milk, coconut milk, and coconut flesh to the boil. Allow to cool somewhat. Beat the egg yolk with the sugar until creamy, add the cooled milk mixture to it, and whisk thoroughly. Place in a non-stick saucepan over a very low heat and stir with a wooden spoon until the custard mix starts to thicken and coat the back of the spoon. Remove from the heat and add the gelatine. When the custard mix has cooled right down to near room temperature fold in the cream and half-fill 4 large greased ramekins. Cover with clingfilm and refrigerate to set.

Meanwhile, dissolve the jaggery or palm sugar in the water and heat to make a syrup. Reserve.

Wash and drain the rice and bring to the boil in the water with the salt and ginger. Simmer until all the liquid is absorbed and the rice is sticky. Don't let the mixture burn or catch on the bottom. (This may take 20 minutes.) Let the rice cool right down and spoon the rice into the remaining space in the mould on top of the coconut custard.

To serve, unmould the desserts and serve with fresh cream and the jaggery syrup lavishly spooned over them.

Summer Coolers

The brief for summer drinks is essentially drinks that are cooling, lightish and uncomplicated. The thirst-quenching factor is of paramount importance here, so we have, unconstitutionally, given some non-alcoholic coolers here, such as iced coffee (often attempted, seldom executed well) and iced teas. With all things retro being fashionable, we've deemed it the right time to put some traditional cocktails like the Tom Collins on parade, and given you some modern versions of old favourites. In addition, there's a couple of full-on stingers like Depth Charge and the Classic Margarita (which will put hairs on your chests) and a banana milkshake with a difference – one for the child inside all of us. Suffice it to say, these were the major considerations in planning some selections.

As far as wine goes, it can be a confusing experience serving what type with what meals. Thankfully, a lot of the old-school snobbery of wine knowhow has been rejected in favour of the educated consumer's instincts which demand, 'Why can't I have a chilled red burgundy with my fish dish?' And why not? Fortunately, the old divide of white with fish and red with meat no longer applies so rigidly – although you have to use common sense in balancing the flavours and weights of a particular dish. (Only a fool would attempt to match a wine with a hot curry – ice-cold lager is much more appropriate.) Crisp, dry, fruity wines are the most popular choices for the season and top labels chosen are Chardonnays and Sauvignon Blancs.

Chardonnay has become almost over-exposed as a favourite grape variety in the last decade, being France's number one type from which most white burgundies are made. Although it can exhibit flavours from the light vanillas to heavy oaks the current favourites are the non-oaked varieties. It goes well with all salads, pastas, and seafoods as well as rice and meat dishes. If aged it will also complement most cheeses and desserts well. Sauvignon Blanc can be a more acidic wine, with flavours of melon and citrus, and is also excellent with chicken dishes and seafood.

Other popular white grapes and names to look out for include Pinot Blanc, Pinot Grigio (Pinot Gris), Soave, Orvieto and Frascati. One other dry white to watch for is the Muscadet. Over-produced to the point that we tired of it in the eighties it is enjoying something of a renaissance, as is the sometimes disappointing Riesling, another survivor of the boom in mass-produced whites. Modern Rieslings are often from South Africa as much as Alsace. The other great boom is in great white sparkling wines. The French *grande marque* houses all seem to have a hand in foreign vineyards as far afield as California and Australia and often produce great dry sparkling wine at around £9–£10 per bottle that would be a fine offering at any dinner or party and won't bust your budget.

For the darker meats, smoked flavours, and heavier end of the spectrum don't forget the reds: Shiraz (Syrah), Cabernet Sauvignon, and the softer Merlots.

One last recommendation, especially relevant for summer – don't overlook rosé wines. Often a blandish type that has neither the depth of the reds nor the refreshing dryness of the whites, the rosé has hitherto been a hit-and-miss affair. Recently, though, we have tried new labels that have really impressed us – you just have to shop around somewhat and don't necessarily go for the cheapest wine on offer.

For the beer drinker things haven't been this good for decades. Although gassy keg bitters haven't disappeared, the wealth of microbreweries that have grown up nationwide have ensured the British tradition is evolving and growing. We have found some stunning beer in tastings, notably Summer Lightning, which embodies the two great facets of flavour dear to us – the light hoppy refreshing bubbliness of the lager and the smooth barley-malty flavours of the true ale or bitter. To get the two embodied in one beer? . . . Heaven!

People often ask us for the definitive tip for serving summer drinks, and if it's to be stated in a nutshell, the answer is to ensure that the drinks are well chilled. If organizing a party you must ensure that you order plenty of ice, and if chilling in ice bins, place drinks in the ice buckets well before the anticipated serving time.

A note on ice. To most people ice is . . . well, ice . . . but it's not that simple. Water freezes at 0° Celsius. Most ice boxes are not that much colder than that, so your ice will melt more quickly if it's not very cold. What you should do is buy commercially-made ice in a bag and put it in the freezer – this way, it will be much colder and dilute your drink less, while still cooling your drink. Also, ice made in a machine is clear unlike ice in an ice tray, which is cloudy. (Ice made with running water is clear and ice made with still water is cloudy. We could tell you why, but enough is enough – sorry to bore you.) There's nothing worse than warm lagers. Go to it!

Recipes

Nosh Island iced tea

Serves 1

½ part white rum
½ part vodka
½ part Gold Label tequila
½ part gin
½ part Cointreau
1 part lemon juice
½ part sugar syrup
1 tsp egg white, whisked
4 parts ginger ale
a slice of lemon

We have tinkered with this one bigtime. We liked the spirit of this drink but found that cola was too sweet so we have adapted it by replacing the cola with ginger ale.

Method
Shake the spirits, lemon juice, syrup, and egg white and strain into a chilled ice-filled glass. Add the ginger ale and lemon.

Iced tea

Serves 6–8

1 litre bottle Evian or
    Volvic mineral water
4 China tea bags (Twinings
    are good)

To serve
lemon/lime slices
peeled sugar cane
    (optional)

This one doesn't have alcohol. Never mind. We've put it in so that you don't make the mistake of trying to use boiling water on tea to infuse it for iced tea. If you do, the drink stews and gets tannic and loses its appeal. In the tropics, tea (usually with a slice of fresh citrus) is the way to ensure that the water is actually safe to drink, having being boiled at some stage – try it with a slice of lime squeezed in, and experiment with different teas, such as Earl Grey.

Method
It is important to use a low-salt mineral water that will not taint the flavours.

Take a bottle of the mineral water, pour out ¼ teacup to make space, and poke the tea bags into the bottle. Put the top on and shake. Leave in the fridge for at least 12 hours then remove the tea bags. You will have fab iced tea, and you can add a slice of lemon or lime and sugar or sugar cane to taste.

Iced coffee

It seems to be more popular in the Mediterranean than in England, but remains one of our top tipples for quenching the thirst and revving up the nervous system on a hot, lazy afternoon.

Method

Make a strong brew of your favourite coffee in a filter machine or a cafetière (a filter machine is better, as you will get no sediment). As soon as it's made pour over lots of ice – you must cool the brew down as soon as possible to stop the coffee stewing. This will, of course, dilute the coffee but if you make it strong enough it will be perfect. Use very cold (preferably commercially made) ice from the deep freeze, not the fridge ice box – you will then need less ice to do the job and your coffee will be stronger.

Serves 1

End-of-the-pier

2 parts Pimm's No. 1

1 part gin

4 or 5 parts chilled 7-Up or
ginger ale (it's up to you
how much you use)

juice of ¼ lime

a long slice of cucumber
(sliced from top to toe
with a potato peeler
into a long strip)

This is a revved-up Pimm's and is much better than the silly salad-in-a-drink that is normally served with one measure of Pimm's to 10 gallons of lemonade.

Method

Take a tall glass, put in some ice, add all the liquid ingredients, and last of all, add the strip of cucumber . . . and don't fall off the pier!

End-of-the-pier

Classic margarita

**Serves 8 guests
or 2 Noshes**

400ml lemon juice
125ml lime juice
1 litre tequila (Gold Label
    is best)
150ml Triple Sec

As well as accompanying the dishes served, drinks play an important part as a social lubricant. This classic margarita is a supercharged way to start the occasion. You'll note that we have omitted the salt rim on the glass. It's a matter of personal preference, so do as you feel. But remember, when people ask us for advice on how to cure hangovers, we reply, 'We don't cure 'em, we give 'em.'

Method
Mix the lemon and lime juice, then mix all the ingredients together in a jug. Place ice into glasses and pour the mixture over the ice. After the second glass, you'll be well on your way!

Bay Breeze and Sea Breeze

Serves 1

2 parts vodka
4 parts cranberry (Classic)
    juice
juice of ½ lime
1½ parts grapefruit or
    pineapple juice

This a simple long drink and ideal for the summer. It also looks very appetizing and has been one of the the most popular cocktails in the current season. The difference between a Sea Breeze and a Bay Breeze is the juice. Grapefruit juice makes a Sea Breeze OK.

Method
Add ice to a long glass, then the vodka, cranberry juice, lime juice and last of all, slowly, the grapefruit or pineapple juice onto the top. This will add a milky look to the drink – and then it's ready!

Summer Nosh

Tom Collins

Serves 1

2 parts gin
½ part sugar syrup
1 part lemon juice
5 parts soda water
4 chunks of very cold ice

As we were looking back through our 'retro' drinks lists, we found this was one that passed muster. A nice change from gin and tonic, it is really refreshing on a hot day. Close your eyes and imagine you're on your tea plantation!

Method
Shake all the ingredients together and pour into a cold cocktail glass.

Depth Charge

A 75cl bottle should provide at least 20 shots

1 bottle sake, warm
Japanese beer (Asahi is
    good), cold

This is a fab novelty . . . it can get messy, so what could be better?

Method
Fill a small shot glass to the top with the sake. Pour the beer into a large glass, only filling it three-quarters full. Lower the shot glass into the beer quickly and drink! The glass may foam over the top, so drink quickly – it's fun.

Banana alcoshake

Serves 1

3 scoops premier quality
    vanilla ice-cream
300ml semi-skimmed milk
1 ripe (not overripe)
    banana
1 part Liqueur de Banane

This one brings out the child inside – with an adult kick to it! Experiment with milkshakes and various permutations of alcohol. You can convince yourself that it's a healthy vitamin-packed drink . . .

Method
Whizz till combined and drink . . . yum!!

Bacardi orange punch

Serves 1

2 parts Bacardi
    (if you can get Gold,
    all the better)
1 part Cointreau
3 parts freshly squeezed
    orange juice
3 parts chilled lemonade

Occasionally, you want a 'long' drink that is smooth and packs a little punch. Citrus juices and rum is a marriage made in heaven – here's one to try from the comfort of your own deckchair.

Method
Shake all the ingredients together, stir, and pour over very cold ice in a tall glass.

Bugger off – I've had enough!

Serves 1

½ part Baileys
1 small espresso coffee
    (made strong)
½ part dark Crème de
    Cacao

This is a type of drinks first aid and is for guests that are fun but want to go home early (mean bastards) and need reviving. It's dedicated to our old mate, Bill Knott. When Bill is around, things generally go a bit haywire, so a drink with inbuilt caffeine is probably not a bad thing.

Method
Pour the Baileys into the espresso, add the Crème de Cacao, stir, and serve. Let's hope your guest asks for another later on.

Going for a Dip

As British people become more travelled they tend to be braver about trying new things. Since the sixties we've seen the popularity of Mexican foods (the tortilla chip and salsa dip being the nineties equivalent of the sixties potato-crisp-and-cheese dip).

The manufacturers have tried to follow this trend and established a huge ready-made market for the hummus, avocado, and taramasalata dips that now spill off our supermarket shelves, but more often than not they are hair cream, with a dash of Swarfega and a sprinkling of grit masquerading as herbs. All smoothly blended, blanded and branded. Sad and never quite good enough. But with a little time, some enthusiasm, and good oils, spices, and ripe ingredients, you too can make a winning guacamole, successful dip, or memorable salad dressing! Again, experiment and try combinations that may sound mad but taste delicious!

In this section, we have revisited old ground and planted a few new seeds to fertilize your imagination for finishing off salads and the like. Apologies if we've omitted your favourites, but we might just do a book on dressings and dips – we love 'em!

Recipes

Bloody Mary dip with horseradish

300ml CLASSIC SALSA
    (page 130)
2 tbsp hot horseradish
    (to taste)
a dash (about 2 tbsp) of
    good vodka
2 tbsp good olive oil

Don't you just love foods that have alcohol in? It's a good excuse, we think.

Method
Combine all the ingredients. Adding the olive oil will give the dip a smooth texture and a shine.

Tomato and red pepper salsa

Serves 4

2 long green chillies
2 red peppers
2 large ripe tomatoes,
    skinned, cored, seeded,
    and chopped
4 large spring onions
    (including flags), finely
    chopped
a handful of chopped
    coriander leaves
3 tbsp fresh-squeezed lime
    juice
1 tbsp olive oil
½ tsp Maldon sea salt

To serve
nachos

Here's a variation on the theme of the classic salsa. The red pepper gives it some extra body and sweetens it slightly.

Method
Roast the chillies and peppers over the hottest part of the grill and turn them until they're evenly charred. Cover them with clingfilm in a bowl until cool then peel away the skin, remembering not to touch your face with your hands. Coarsely chop them.

Stir together all the ingredients in a large bowl and refrigerate for 1 hour if possible. Adjust the seasoning and serve with nachos, for dipping in the salsa.

 **Going for a Dip**

Chargrilled sweetcorn and black bean salsa

Serves 4

6 tbsp black beans, soaked
    overnight and drained
1 red pepper
about 3 cobs chargrilled
    sweetcorn
150ml CLASSIC SALSA
    (page 130)

Made using the basic salsa recipe, this is a more filling salsa that can also be a side dish. You can, if desired, mix this with a little mayonnaise and fill pitta pockets with the mixture for an easy-to-carry picnic idea.

Method
Cook the beans in salted water on a medium simmer for about 30 minutes and then on a low simmer for another 25 minutes until tender. Drain and cool. Roast the pepper over the hottest part of the grill and turn it until it's evenly charred. Cover with clingfilm in a bowl until cool then peel away the skin, then core it and cut it into fine dice. Shuck the cobs of their sweetcorn kernels with a very sharp knife and combine with the beans and pepper. Add just enough salsa to wet the mixture – it should be stiff and robust, not sloppy. This version is great with wedges of grilled floury tortillas that have a thin layer of Monterey Jack (or Cheddar is OK) sandwiched between two layers of tortilla.

Mint vinaigrette

Maldon sea salt and freshly
    ground black pepper
1 jar mint sauce
6 tbsp extra virgin olive oil

This is a bit of a cheat idea – but then Nick always looks for new and easy to make innovations. We took some pre-prepared mint sauce, which is rather vinegary, and adapted it into something of quality by simply adding a premier olive oil. It was that easy!

Method
Mix to make a dressing to dress grilled lamb chops.

Roasted-garlic aïoli

A variation on the garlic mayo theme. Roasting the garlic bulb seems like a bother, but it really does transform the flavour (just as a slow-roasted onion becomes sweet, so does the humble garlic clove). Roast up half a dozen bulbs at a time – they keep well in olive oil and flavour the oil very subtly as a bonus.

Method

Roast 2 whole bulbs (to produce about 12 cloves), on a barbecue with the kettle lid on for about 15 minutes or so on medium hot heat, or in a domestic oven preheated to 220°C/425°F/gas mark 7 for about 15–20 minutes. This will soften and sweeten the cloves. When cool enough to handle they can easily be squeezed out of their papery skins and into the basic mayonnaise recipe on page 21. Mix well. This will make a smoother-tasting aïoli than using raw garlic.

Seafood sauce

½ tsp freshly ground
    black pepper
1 tsp dry (yellow
    powdered) mustard
1½ tsp Maldon sea salt
1 tbsp tequila
3 tsp fresh lime juice
2 tsp Cointreau
juice and grated zest of
    2 medium oranges
4 egg yolks
300ml corn oil
Maldon sea salt and freshly
    ground black pepper

An unusual version of a seafood sauce using tequila. Again, we do like putting booze into food whenever we can. If you see people shooting small glasses of this one and then biting down on a prawn, you'll know it's our recipe!

Method

Combine all the ingredients (except the oil and seasonings) in a processor and blend until smooth. Keeping the machine running on full power, pour in the oil in a reasonably quick, smooth stream. Check seasonings and adjust as necessary. This will keep in a plastic covered container for 3 days. It also makes a good dip for crudités.

Harissa sauce

60g dried hot chillies
4 cloves garlic
1 skinned, deseeded, very
    fine diced tomato
2 tbsp ground cumin
2 tbsp toasted cumin seeds
1 tsp salt
8 tbsp virgin olive oil

Every North African country has its own version – the Moroccan is milder than the Algerian, the Tunisian is hot, and by the time you get to Libya they have to strap you down to spoon it into your mouth.

Method

The time-honoured way is to blend all the ingredients with a pestle and mortar. If you have one and can spare the time, so be it – hand-ground produce always seems more worthwhile if only for the

sacrifice! Lazy people can always use the blender.

Makes 250ml

Coconut chutney

3 green chillies, deseeded
    and chopped coarsely
½ tsp fresh grated ginger
    root
1 small shallot, finely sliced
130ml whole yogurt
2 tsp finely chopped onion
3 tbsp coconut oil
6 fresh or 2 tsp dried curry
    leaves
1 tsp mustard seeds
130ml fresh water
120g fresh coconut, finely
    grated

This goes well with most Indian-style foods and particularly with Bombay potatoes and crisp dosa pancakes. Poppadums usually go with a mango chutney but this is a nice alternative. This is a fresh chutney but it will keep for 3 days in a cold fridge.

Method

In a blender/food processor purée the chillies, ginger, and shallot, and blend in the yogurt. Fry the onion until golden in the coconut oil, add the curry leaves and the mustard seeds, and fry them until they begin to pop. Add the water and coconut and stir until warm, and season to taste – do not let the coconut brown. Remove from the heat and allow to cool. The texture you should try to achieve is moist but not wet.

Fresh tomato marmalade

Makes 1 litre

2.5 kg firm, ripe plum
    tomatoes, in 1cm dice
700g granulated sugar
100ml white wine vinegar
30ml balsamic vinegar
½–1 tbsp Maldon sea salt
½–1 tsp ground white
    pepper

In a tied muslin bag
1 tsp black mustard seeds
20 whole allspice
12 whole cloves
6 whole cardamons
4 dried chillies
10 basil leaves
2 dried bay leaves

Tomato marmalade goes well with cheeses and has a distinctive sharp flavour. Tomatoes in Britain have a reputation for being bland, being picked when unripe and exported to the UK green, so use ripe plum tomatoes for this one.

Method

Place all the ingredients in a stainless-steel pot and bring slowly to the boil, stirring frequently to dissolve the sugar, then simmer very gently over the lowest flame for 30 minutes. Strain into a bowl using a slotted spoon, reserving the flesh and keeping the tomato juices in the pan. Return the spice bag to the pan and simmer over a low heat for 2–2½ hours or until the juices have reduced to about 10 per cent of their original volume and have a syrupy flow. Then fold the reserved tomato flesh into the syrup and when well mixed pour the hot mixture into clean sterile jars. Seal with a disc of greaseproof paper and an airtight lid.

Warm honey dressing

Serves 8

2 large pinches Maldon
    sea salt
4 tbsp raspberry or cider
    vinegar
4 tbsp clear honey
    (a strong one like
    Greek Mountain or
    Australian is good)
8 tbsp virgin olive oil
freshly ground black
    pepper

Here is a foolproof and great-tasting dressing that doesn't need any difficult measuring. You'll need to watch one thing – that the mixture doesn't overheat in the saucepan. Too hot, and the mixture will split, and then it's difficult to get it right again without starting over.

Method

Dissolve the salt in the vinegar, then stir in the honey, and add the oil and stir. Season with plenty of black pepper. Warm the dressing up on a very low heat in a saucepan.

Classic vinaigrette

Maldon sea salt
1 tbsp vinegar
freshly ground black
    pepper
4 tbsp virgin olive oil

The main thing to remember is that salt does not dissolve in oil, so dissolve the salt in the vinegar first. You can vary the types of vinegar according to personal preference, choosing cider, wine, or whatever you please, but always use good ingredients to maximize results.

Method

Whisk the salt in the vinegar, add some black pepper and stir briskly, then pour in the oil in a steady stream.

If the vinaigrette is for a fish dish, lemon juice may be substituted for the sharpness of the vinegar.

Sun-dried tomato dressing

Sun-dried tomatoes were the kiwi fruit of the late eighties and early nineties. Overused and now much abused they have fallen into disrepute as far as the cutting edge of new cuisine is concerned. This is really a pity, as they had a great density of flavour. We feel it's time to give them a break and allot them some parole time for good behaviour.

Method

As the classic vinaigrette (above) but with the addition of 4 sun-dried tomatoes, finely chopped, per teacup of dressing. Leave the dressing to mingle flavours for at least 30 minutes before you serve it.

Fruit dressing

Make as a basic vinaigrette, but substitute freshly squeezed orange juice for the oil then add 1 tsp of grainy mustard, 1 tsp of honey, and the zest of 1 orange. Variations and combinations can be made with lemons and limes. This dressing goes well with salads where a large proportion of bitter leaves are used (e.g. radicchio or endive), and with warm salads of duck and grilled or smoked fish.

Conversion Tables

These are practical conversions for use in the kitchen.
Dry spoon measures in the book are rounded or heaped, not level.

Dry measure

Metric	Imperial
g	*oz*
8	¼
15	½
30	1
60	2
90	3
120	4
140	5
175	6
200	7
225	8
250	9
285	10
450	16
	lb
675	1½
900	2
kg	
1	2¼
1.5	3½
2	4½
2.3	5

Liquid measure

Metric	Imperial	
ml	*fl oz*	*tsp*
5	–	1
10	–	2
		tbsp
20	–	1
25	1	1½
50	2	3
75	3	4
100	4	–
		pints
150	5	¼
175	6	–
200	7	–
250	8	⅓
300	10	½
400	14	⅔

Metric	Imperial	
ml	*fl oz*	*pints*
450	15	¾
500	16	–
575	20	1
700	25	1¼
750	27	–
850	30	1½
900	32	1⅔
litres		
1	35	1¾
1.1	40	2
1.5	50	2¼
1.75	60	3
2	72	3½
2.25	84	4
9	320	16

Index